"After overcom[ing barcode] it
into this valu[able book, you'll find an emo]-
tionally invol[ving and intellectually challenging]
message. Reco[mmended.]
— Roger E. Herman, CSP, CMC
author, *Keeping Good People* and
other management books

"A fascinating story that is chock full of hands-on, practical, and down-to-earth common sense. I recommend it to all who want to do their best—and get results. Delightful reading."
— Joe Batten, Chairman, Batten Associates
author, *Tough-Minded Leadership*, *The Master Motivator*, and *The Leadership Principles of Jesus*

"*Bubba* shows the impact managers' actions and systems have on people and organizational results. The concepts transform operating philosophies from theory to practical day-to-day application. We've applied the concepts and they work!"
— Jim Ball, Director of Human Resources
PI, Inc.

"Bubba is right on! He's one smart guy. We all could learn a lot by listening to the common-sense wisdom of the 'Bubbas' in our own organizations!"
— Barbara "BJ" Hateley, co-author,
A Peacock in the Land of Penguins:
A Tale of Diversity and Discovery

"Practical wisdom about what's wrong with our workplaces—and how to fix it."
— John Case, author, *Open Book Management*
and *The Open-Book Experience*
Editor-at-Large, *Inc.* magazine

"A great book to make us realize we should focus on the positive aspects of people and create work environments for them. Trust me—this is a must-read book if you want to be a change agent in your place of work."
— John Hull, Vice President, Sourcing
EJ Footwear

"If you want a fun read and plan only one business book this decade, this is it."
—Gary Fellers, author, *Creativity for Leaders*

"Entertaining and informative. 'Bubba' can help you improve poorly designed system processes, leadership, and your ability to tap the knowledge and expertise of your workers."
— Dr. William H. Hendrix, Professor of Management
Clemson University; Chairman, The 21st Century Organizational Excellence Awards

"Bubba is the American 'Everyman,' and Dennis Melton and David Dunn have shown the way for the anonymous Bubbas in the business world."
— Steven F. Hayward, author,
Churchill on Leadership

"The difference between reaching a company's potential and just talking about it, is the commitment to leading the 95% and not reacting to the 5%. *Bubba* does a great job of teaching managers how to do it!"
— Larry Kipp, Jr., Operations Manager
TRW-Vehicle Safety Systems, Inc.

"*Bubba on Business* is a real gem . . . a 'must read' for every manager and team leader. It captures the essence of leadership principles and offers practical, down-to-earth tools to achieve a positive and productive work environment . . . plus, it's a lot of fun to read!"
— Cher Holton, PhD, CSP, CMC
The Holton Consulting Group, Inc.
co-author, *The Manager's Short Course*

"Melton and Dunn spin an instructive tale about the application of common sense to everyday performance problems across a wide range of organizations. It's an easy down-home read with a payoff that reaches uptown issues. Here are the keys to the power of respect and responsibility and a warning about the risk of expecting only compliance with the rules."
— Larry L. Axline, Chief Operating Officer
Holt Consulting Services, Inc.

"Why is it so hard for those of us in business to remember that success depends on people, not rules and policies? Bubba walks right out of the pages into real life where managers live everyday. Try his principles; they work!"
— Mike Stubblefield
Director, Structures, North & South America
Johnson Controls Inc.

"Yo! Listen up! The new business Everyman is here! Hubba, hubba . . . here comes Bubba! And not a moment too soon! *Bubba on Business* offers sage advice for a zany time."
— Louis Patler, co-author,
If It Ain't Broke. . . .Break It!

BUBBA on BUSINESS

Common sense from working people about respect, accountability, and results

Dennis W. Melton

David C. Dunn

BUBBA on BUSINESS

Common sense from working people about respect, accountability, and results

Dennis W. Melton

David C. Dunn

Select Press
Corte Madera, CA

Copyright 1998 by Dennis W. Melton and David C. Dunn

All rights reserved. No part of this publication may be reproduced, distributed, or transmitted in any form or by any means, including photocopying, recording, digital, online, or other electronic or mechanical methods, without the prior written permission of the publisher, except in the case of brief quotations embodied in critical reviews and certain other noncommercial uses permitted by copyright law. For permission requests, write to the publisher, addressed "Attention: Permissions Coordinator," at the address below.

Select Press
P.O. Box 37
Corte Madera, CA 94976-0037
(415) 435-4461

Bubba on Business: Common Sense from Working People about Respect, Accountability, and Results / Dennis W. Melton and David C. Dunn

ISBN 1-890-777-03-X

Printed in the United States of America
10 9 8 7 6 5 4 3 2 1

Contents

"Folks ain't opposed to change, when they see what's in it for them." —Bubba

Preface   ix

Thanks   xi

Seeing the Impact   1
The workplace is a system. But who is it designed for, and what results does it produce?

Bubba Speaks Up   9
Arbitrary rules designed to stop a few malicious people more often actually "catch" good employees.

Pursuing Change   19
The vast majority can see the symptoms created by a flawed system. It's up to leaders to listen and then plot a different course.

A Curve in the Road   27
Change, for people and companies, is a process that begins with seeing the problem and understanding the consequences.

Redesigning the System   43
Traditional systems rely on rules that specify the worst we'll tolerate. Effective workplaces set expectations and develop accountability by involving the 95%.

Great Expectations   53
Leaders have to set the direction and ask for buy-in from their people.

Taking It Personally 63
You build trust by doing what's right, one situation at a time.

Winners and Losers 75
As Einstein said, the definition of insanity is to do the same thing over and over and expect different results.

Ensuring Accountability 87
Treating people with respect means expecting them to act like adults—and confronting problems immediately and directly.

Making a Difference 97
Expect changes to be challenged . . . your response communicates your commitment.

Getting Results 113
It takes time and effort to create change, but staying the same guarantees failure.

Final Thoughts 121

Appendix A: But What About . . . ? 123

Appendix B: Case Studies 127

Appendix C: Measurable Results 131

Appendix D: Ways to Get Started 133

Who Wrote This Book? 137

Preface

This book is about achieving business results in partnership with people—people like Bubba.

Bubba is everyone

The central factor in this story, as in any real organization, is 'Bubba.' Some may view the name Bubba as derogatory; a term, like "redneck" or "hick," intended to poke fun at working people, especially Southerners. Nothing could be farther from our intent. We like Bubba. We respect him (and her!) and we know that Bubba is the one who really makes any business successful.

"Bubba" describes a perspective, not a stereotype. Bubba is a fictional stand in for the great majority of people—those who work hard, care enough to get frustrated, and do their best in most situations. In this book, Bubba is a technician in a manufacturing plant, but Bubba can be found in every office, hospital, shop, and retail store.

Workers' wisdom through storytelling

Rather than write a typical business book, we've woven a fictional story, based on real incidents, that illustrates the process of making the workplace better. We've marked a few of the more unbelievable actual situations and comments with an asterisk (*). Naturally, we changed names, places and enough details to protect anyone from embarrassment. Most importantly, the results described are real. They can be—and have been—achieved by any organization that is willing to act on the principles outlined in Bubba's story.

Change your organizational culture

The process we describe involves shaping workplace culture—the system that governs how people get things done at work. The system includes the personalities, behaviors, and skills of people; the policies and the practices; the decision-making processes; the communication channels; and the informal ways "things are around here."

Every organization has a culture that either inhibits or enables positive business results. Cultures can be shaped through some simple, practical techniques that get dramatic results.

We believe that Bubba and the vast majority of working people are keen observers of how the workplace really operates. Bubba's "wisdom" comes from real-world experience. Unfortunately, most managers don't take time to listen to Bubba, and thus miss a vital source of ideas and opinions—not to mention support for business results. This wisdom, what we call "Bubba on Business," is the key to improved business results.

Dennis W. Melton
David C. Dunn

Thanks

To God, without Whose divine intervention our partnership and this book would never have been.

To our wives, Julia Dunn and Ginger Melton, without whom our work and travel would be overwhelming: Thank you for making our homes a haven. To our kids, Rebekah and David Dunn, Jr. and Laura and Matthew Melton: Thanks for thinking we are special.

To our parents, Sonny and Jo Dunn and Wade and Delline Melton. Your love, sacrifices, hard work, and common sense teaching laid the foundation for our lives and for this book.

To Mike McDermott and Ed Rachie, original partners in Ninety-Five/Five, who laid the foundation of the 95/5 philosophy.

A special thanks to Sheldon Bowles (co-author of Raving Fans and Gung Ho!) for his interest in Bubba, and to Rick and Carolynn Crandall of Select Press. We appreciate the time, energy, and enthusiastic support they devoted to making *Bubba on Business* better.

Finally, we extend our sincerest thanks and appreciation to our clients, too numerous to mention individually. It is their openness, passion for making things better, commitment to the 95/5 principles, and willingness to listen to their own "Bubbas" that has created positive workplaces for their employees.

Seeing the Impact

The workplace is a system. But who is it designed for, and what results does it produce?

* * * * *

"Most people want to do what's right, but they get fed up." —Bubba

---

1

Wham! The break room door nearly came unhinged and Bubba Self jumped three inches out of his seat as the press crew entered. It sounded like a riot. Mingled snatches of conversation and hard-core profanity reached Bubba, but he could only catch phrases. One thing was certain: The crew was mad!

"Two hours overtime every day!"

"And Saturday on top of that! They can't do this!"

"I always thought Sonny was one of us, and now he's. . . !"

"I can't work over . . . I got class tonight."

"Well, I guess they'll just send you home. That's what they do when you try your best around here."

a safety violation—and they sure don't like mandatory overtime. But that's what the policy says. I reckon you have to enforce the policy, or there isn't any point in having one, right? It's Management 101—you have to treat everyone exactly the same; no exceptions."

"Yeah, I guess that's the way you have to look at it," he replied half-heartedly. Marty looked directly at him. "How often have you had to write up somebody when you didn't think it was fair?"

"More than I want to," Sonny said. "But this was for Sam's own good, too. I mean, double-loading a die on the press is dangerous. He could have been hurt, and he could have damaged the tool. Maybe he didn't do it on purpose, but if somebody breaks a rule, they have to be punished. We can't play favorites. I'll bet Sam will remember this for a long time."

"Yeah," Marty said. "That's what I'm afraid of. Will Sam remember how important safety is, or how we treated him—an employee with a spotless record?"

"If we made an exception for Sam, some jerk would claim we have to make one for him, too," Sonny said.

> Do rules for the jerks mean the jerks rule?

"But why do we let the jerk drive our decisions?" Marty asked. "A jerk who's been this close to being fired every year for 10 years, but just keeps slipping through loopholes?"

"Yeah, but Marty, we write the jerks up, too. It just don't do any good. They don't mind being written up. All we can do is follow the rules," Sonny replied. "We don't make 'em. Look, if we don't follow the rules, the jerks will be running the place."

And that, Marty decided as he jotted in his daybook, was precisely what was happening:

> The jerks are winning -- good people pay the price.
>
> Sometimes the system creates unintended consequences.

Marty's Daybook

3

The next afternoon, Henry and Earl were talking quietly at their work stations as Bubba approached.

"What's going on?" Bubba asked. Earl snickered, choked back a laugh, then erupted.

"Earl saw Jimmy at lunch," Henry responded, tight-lipped with disapproval.

"But Jimmy's out today—again," Bubba said.

"I know," said Henry, obviously unamused. "He showed up at the smoking area after lunch. Tell him, Earl."

"You better keep this to yourself, you hear!" Earl whispered. "He just said to be watching at the time clock 10 minutes before quitting time."

Sure enough, at the appointed hour, Jimmy showed up at the time clock outside Sonny's office.

"Jimmy, where in blazes have you been?" demanded Sonny. "You didn't call in again. You knew if you had one more point on your attendance, we'd have to fire you." Jimmy slowly reached into the rack for his timecard, inserted it in the clock, and handed it to Sonny with a sly smile.

"Sorry I'm late, boss," Jimmy drawled. It took a moment for Sonny to realize that, by clocking in late instead of missing the whole day—even seven hours, 50 minutes late—Jimmy would only receive half a point under the attendance system and would keep his job. And one point would come off tomorrow—it had been 30 days since his last warning.* He'd played the system and won again. Sonny's face began pulsating like a faulty neon sign.

"Just get . . . get over there and get to work!" Sonny stammered, struggling to control his language if not his emotions. "At least you'll be working two hours over tonight with everybody else!"

> Beating the system is a game to some: "I win, you lose."

"I can't work over tonight. I have bowling league. Besides," Jimmy said pleasantly, "the rule says we have to get four hours' notice or it ain't mandatory. I hate to let you

---

* Asterisks indicate actual situations and comments encountered by the authors (with names and details changed to protect individuals' identities).

down, but I didn't get four hours' notice." With that, Jimmy ambled to his work area, giving a wave to Marty who was watching from his office.

Watching this, Bubba wondered if he should talk to Marty. He didn't want to make Marty angry. "But," he thought, "if this don't show there's a problem, what will?"

Bubba Speaks Up

Arbitrary rules designed to stop a few malicious people more often actually "catch" good employees.

* * * * *

"I hope you don't think I'm out of line, but I don't think it's fair to start with." —Bubba

4

Marty looked up to see Bubba standing silently just outside the door. Bubba seemed nervous, his fingers gripping the brim of the cap he held in his hand. No knock; no greeting—just standing there.

"What can I do for you, Bubba?" Marty said tiredly. He glanced at the clock and saw that Bubba's shift had just ended. "Oh, I don't need you to stay over; just operators and packers. You can go on home."

"No, sir, that ain't what this is about," Bubba said. "I don't mean to stick my nose in where it ain't welcome, but I came to talk to you about Sam."

"Oh," said Marty, remembering the discomfort of suspending Sam. "Come on in and sit down, but I can't talk about a personnel situation involving another employee. That wouldn't be fair to him."

"Well, I hope you don't think I'm out of line, but I don't think it's fair to start with," Bubba said. "Now, I know you can't really discuss it, but I need to say some things just for me. And the thing that's got me upset is that this was Sam's first problem since he come to work here. Marty, how long you been knowing me?"

Marty sat back. Bubba had been one of the first operators he met when he transferred to this plant nearly 10 years ago. Bubba was smart and committed, and everybody seemed to listen to him. Marty had recommended that Bubba train as a technician, and he'd made a good one. He just had a sense about how to handle things. "Ever since I got here, Bubba," he said.

Advice worth listening to

"I like workin' for you, Marty," said Bubba. "But I have to tell you that I think you did wrong suspending Sam. He made an honest mistake, and he's losing three days' pay for it. Meantime, there's folks like Jimmy that have been causin' trouble for years, and they're still workin'."

As Bubba mentioned Jimmy, a cold chill ran down Marty's back. And it wasn't just the incident moments before. Jimmy had been disciplined, suspended, and chewed out countless times. But it didn't do any good. He seemed to enjoy confronting Marty and the supervisors—as if his mission in life were to stay in management's face. Like today, just when Sonny had a fleeting hope that they had him, Jimmy would find some loophole to get out of it. Or he'd do better just long enough to have the violation removed from his file, and then do it all over again. It was as if rules and policies were written for Jimmy's personal benefit!

"The way I see it, there's just a few around here causing the real problems," Bubba continued, "but the majority—like Sam—has to pay for them."

Marty opened his daybook and penned a note.

> Small minority causes most problems

"Bubba, you know I can't talk specifically about Sam or Jimmy, but what percent of our folks would you say really seem to cause problems over and over?"

Bubba looked surprised. "Marty, you know 'em as well as I do. Chuck and Barb are the worst ones to miss work. And Jimmy . . . well, you know all about him. Harold and Missy are here most days, but they're late two or three times a week, and they always seem to have a problem with production or quality. They keep me back there all the time, saying their machines ain't right. I'd say it's less than 10% of the people—maybe about 5%."

Marty added to his note:

> Small minority causes most problems -- about 5 percent of people

Bubba chuckled. "I remember ol' Fred Harrison used to be a problem, too."

"Yeah, but we let him go," Marty interjected.

"After 15 years!" replied Bubba. "And the only reason you got him then was 'cause he lost count of how many days he could miss before his last warning dropped off.*"

Milking the system

Marty was stunned. "You mean, people actually track how many days they have to wait before missing again?"

"Why, sure," said Bubba, a bit shocked at Marty's surprise. "Barb's even got a calendar at her machine with the next day she can miss circled in red ink!* You never seen that?" Marty had to admit he'd never looked.

"Barb and Missy not only know their own attendance, they know everybody else's attendance. They even take turns missing sometimes.* They're geniuses at finding ways around the rules. If they spent as much energy working as they do figuring ways to get out of work, they'd own this place by now."

People notice

"If it's only about 5%, why does it seem we have more problems than that?" Marty asked.

"Because people notice what happens—who gets by and who gets nailed," Bubba said. "People say, 'Well, if they can lay out or goof off, I will, too.' Most people want to do what's right, but they get fed up." Bubba lowered his voice. "Like what happened to Sam. Marty, I think you ought to call Sam in and warn him, then bring him back. He won't do it no more. The rest of us would appreciate it."

"Will they?" Marty asked. "If I let Sam get by, everybody will want to get by one time. Everybody'd shout, Favoritism!"

"Wait a minute," said Bubba. "Everybody? Who do you think would be the first ones wantin' to get by with something? It's those same ones we talked about, the 5%. And besides, who do you think that rule was put in for, anyway?"

Marty thought a minute. "Well, it was to protect everybody. It's safety."

Bubba shook his head. "No. Matter of fact, I know who it was put in for. Ol' girl named Martha used to work here. She was the most careless person I ever seen. She'd double-load the press about twice a week. I think it was just to tear something up so's she could stand around. It didn't bother her one bit if she cracked a die or broke a bolt. So finally they put in this rule to stop her from doing it."

"Did it work?" asked Marty.

"Yeah; stopped her from that trick, but she kept finding new ways to screw stuff up. She'd put stuff in backward, or she'd have such bad quality it would take us half a day to sort through her parts. She'd say that production was too high, or the material was bad—you know, any excuse."

"So, we put in a rule for somebody who was screwing up over and over, and then applied it to somebody else who made one mistake," Marty thought aloud as he wrote:

> Rules written for 5% -- applied to everyone
> -----
> Rules don't stop the 5%.
>
> but punish others
> -----
> 5% play the system to their benefit

Marty looked up. "Bubba, you've given me something to think about. I don't know what I can do about Sam at this point. I can't just change a rule. I'll talk to Human Resources, then I'll call Sam. But I want to think some more about the issue of who the rules were written for, and who they get applied to. I know that doesn't seem right, but we have to treat everybody equal."

"Why should we?" Bubba asked as he stood to leave. "Seems to me we ought to treat people according to how they act."

Then Marty captured Bubba's parting sentiment in his daybook:

> *When you give better, you ought to get better.*

5

"Pull up a stool, Bubba," called Roy, the bartender at the local watering hole called The Palace. "Mighty quiet this afternoon. The usual suspects ain't showed theirselves yet."

"Most of 'em are pulling some overtime at the plant," Bubba replied. "You ain't seen Sam Blount today, have you?"

"He was in here earlier. Mighty down in the mouth," said Roy. "Said he ain't felt so humiliated since he was a kid. The way he got treated does seem harsh, don't it?"

"Yeah, I think so," said Bubba. He looked at the corner table where Jimmy and some friends were playing cards and drinking, adding quietly, "Especially when folks like that can get by with most anything."

"Uh-huh," Roy agreed. "Hey, Jimmy, you been in here about all day. Don't you have to work?" he called out.

Jimmy laughed as he ambled over to the bar where Bubba sat. "Well, I did work, didn't I, Bubba? For about five minutes," he said. "I just wanted to jerk ol' Sonny's chain a little. Keeps him straight. Besides, I don't like to kiss up to nobody. You know what I mean, Bubba?"

"No," Bubba replied simply. Jimmy's hand rested uncomfortably on Bubba's shoulder, but he resisted the impulse to slap it off. Just then, Bubba's brother Junior walked in. Jimmy moved his hand and nodded in greeting.

"I'll bet you were in there talking to your buddy Marty about me, or maybe poor ol' Sam," Jimmy said with mock sympathy. "You know, it's pitiful how they treated old Sam. I been telling you for years that sooner or later management will get you. See, my idea is that if you screw up enough, they'll quit messing with you."

"Well, you set a high standard for the rest of us," Bubba said. Roy choked back a guffaw, but Jimmy didn't laugh. "Tell me, how can you afford to be out of work so much when you ain't getting paid?"

> Most rules define the level of misbehavior you will tolerate, rather than setting a high standard.

"I just ain't for sale to no company that don't respect me," Jimmy said stiffly. "If they'd pay more, I'd consider being there more."

Bubba ignored the stupidity of this logic and pressed, "So why don't you quit?"

"Cause I'm having too much fun driving people like you crazy!" Jimmy laughed, slapping Bubba's back and walking away. "What would you have to talk about? They can't fire me. See you around, Mr. Company Man!" he mocked.

The 5% are everywhere

Junior sat down beside Bubba. "Junior, y'all got any like him over where you work?" Bubba asked.

"They're everywhere, ain't they?" Junior replied as he poured his beer into a glass.

"But y'all have a union. Ain't that supposed to make it better for the workers?"

"Not when it comes to people like Jimmy. My job as steward is to make sure the company follows the contract and don't take advantage of the workers. But, between you and I, it seems like I spend more time trying to get screw-ups like him off the hook than helping people who deserve it," Junior said. "Most of the people and most of the supervisors are no trouble. But there's a few—workers and supervisors, too—just like him that make everybody miserable."

"Yeah, I was talking about that with Marty. He was asking about how many of our folks really cause trouble, and I figured it was about 5%, more or less," said Bubba.

Junior thought a minute. "Yeah, that's about right. Now, you've got a few ol' boys who will see what they can get away with once in awhile. But there ain't many ringleaders."

"So what do you do about them?" Bubba asked. "They ruin the place for everybody else because most of the rules are made for them."

"When you figure it out, let me know," said Junior, draining his glass, "and we'll sell it! Bring me another one, Roy."

95/5 Principle

- The vast majority of employees are good people.
- A small minority—about 5%—tries to manipulate the system.
- Most systems are designed for the 5% who manipulate them, not the 95% who do their best.

Pursuing Change

*The vast majority can see the
symptoms created by a flawed system.
It's up to leaders to listen and then
plot a different course.*

* * * * *

*"Folks ain't opposed to change, when they
see what's in it for them."* —Bubba

6

A little after nine the next morning, Bubba figured Marty had really lost it.

There was Marty with his little book, writing as he walked. He'd stop and look—at a machine, a stack of boxes, posted notices on the bulletin board, the time clock—then he'd jot a note and mutter to himself. A couple of the guys got a kick out of Marty's actions. Almost everyone seemed in a better mood since Sam had been called back. Even the complainers like Missy seemed glad about the decision. Of course, she may have been happy just to be standing around. Bubba had been listening to her all morning claim her machine wasn't working right—again.

"Wonder what's with him?" Bubba said to Sam, motioning toward Marty.

"I don't know, but he's been this way ever since I got here," Sam said. "I told him I appreciated another chance. By the way, somebody said you went to bat for me, and I really appreciate it."

"Well, I talked to Marty, but he had to handle it from there," Bubba said sheepishly. Just then, Marty walked by, so Bubba figured he'd see what was going on.

"Marty," Bubba called out, trying to catch him.

"Yes, Bubba?" Marty replied, looking up from his daybook.

"I really appreciate what you did for Sam," Bubba said, "but after what you said last night, I wondered how you were going to explain it to the 5%."

"I talked with Marilyn in Human Resources last night. I decided that you were right—the vast majority of people would appreciate us taking into consideration Sam's record. And I really didn't care right then what the 5% thought," Marty said. "After we looked at it, we realized that the length of the suspension was up to three days. I told her we needed to reconsider the policy, but in the meantime, this was one of those 'discretion of management' things. I'll take the heat, 'cause it was the right thing to do."

"So what in thunder are you doing roaming the building like a cat burglar—or a peepin' Tom?" Bubba asked. "Are you checking up on us? We were wondering whether to call a lawyer or the nut farm."

"No, I haven't gone crazy, but I'm finding some things

that might be making us all that way," Marty laughed. "If you have a minute to come to the office, I'll tell you."

"Well, maybe Missy can run without me for just a few minutes," Bubba said sarcastically.

7

"Let me tell you what I've been asking myself," Marty said. "Is high performance rational?"

"Huh?"

"Does it make sense to do your best, as opposed to the bare minimum?" Marty asked. "See, I was up last night thinking. Why is it that the majority seem to get jerked around by the rules put in place for the 5%? So I came in early and started looking for things we do that actually reward the 5% and punish the good performers."

"What in thunder are you talking about?" Bubba asked.

Consequences influence behavior

"Consequences influence people's behavior," Marty explained. "We all naturally do those things that make life easier, and avoid those things that make life harder. Problem is, many of Specialty Products' rules and policies seem to be geared to the 5%, so I wanted to see what kind of consequences people get around here."

"So what'd you find? Bubba asked.

"Look here at my book," Marty said, handing his daybook to Bubba.

> 1) Trust and rules
> 2) Attendance
> 3) Production and quality expectations
> 4) Pay and advancement
> 5) Attention and recognition

"First, look at all the ways that we tell people, 'We can't trust you.' Why do we have time clocks?

> Trust and rules.

Because there are some people who would lie about their time. Does the clock keep people from missing work or being late?" Marty said.

"No, but it's harder to cheat," Bubba said, a little perplexed. "Besides, every place has time clocks. Nobody minds that."

"I'll bet they mind doctor's notes," Marty replied. "How many times have people paid out money for a doctor visit to get a note, just because our policy says you have to have one or you'll get a point. The issue is, we treat everybody like they're in grade school."

"But we have to have rules, or Jimmy and his crowd would shut us down," Bubba objected.

"Have the rules really changed their behavior?" Marty asked. "I've been here 10 years, and Jimmy's always acted the same regardless of how we change the rules. In the meantime, a lot of other good people who don't intend to break the rules get caught. Like Sam did on the press."

"Or like Cathy," Bubba added. "Hadn't missed a day in four years, and then gets wrote up when her kid got in trouble with the law and she had to go to court with him a few times."

"That's what I mean," said Marty. "The rules we have aren't really working. They tell the 95% that we don't trust them, and the 5% just find a way around them. I can think of a dozen examples," Marty said, "but Cathy's example illustrates my second point."

"What do we really want attendance to be?" Marty asked.

Attendance.

"I guess you expect folks to be here every day," Bubba said.

"I thought that, too, but what does our policy say? If you think about it, it says there's a certain amount of time that's OK to miss."

"Well, of course, we have excused absences for sickness . . ."

"With a doctor's note," reminded Marty, "and those can be faked."

"And there's bereavement . . ." continued Bubba.

"Again, with proof of death—and we tell you how much your loved one is worth by specifying how much time you get," Marty interrupted again.

"So?" Bubba asked, wondering where Marty was headed.

"The point is, we say we expect people here, but there's 30 reasons that we'll say it's OK if they aren't," Marty answered. "And if that isn't enough, we have a point system that says you aren't really in trouble until you cross a certain line. That line usually catches only the people who aren't watching, because they don't intend to cross it."

"And folks like Jimmy who want to play games can find a way around it," Bubba added.

"So, again, is it more rewarding to come to work every day, or to try to find that line and get as much time off as you can?" Marty asked. "Now, think about this: Who has it easier—the high performers or those who only do the minimum?"

> Production and quality expectations.

Bubba thought about his experience with Missy. Other operators would handle variations in material and changes in design by themselves, but every little deviation drove Missy crying to Bubba: "Bubba, I just can't make this stuff come out right! This piece of junk they gave me won't do right. I can't be responsible for making production if they won't get a new machine . . . or get the right material or quit changing the way they want it done."

What did Missy get for her antics? Well, a lot of Bubba's time, for one. And she got to stand by the machine while he worked on it. If the press supervisor asked her to sweep or make boxes while Bubba worked, she griped. Then she'd sweep for a minute, and off she'd go to the bathroom or the break room.

Meanwhile, when Sonny, the press supervisor, needed something done in a hurry, who got the job? Yep—good old reliable Sam, or Henry if Sam was busy; sometimes Marge or Cathy. Sometimes if all of them were behind, Sonny would do it himself rather than ask Missy to do it. After all, he'd just have to do it over again anyway.

"From a work standpoint, the better performers have it harder," Bubba replied. "They get to do harder work, and more of it. And when things don't go right, who do you get upset with? The good performers."

"I hate to admit it, but I've done it myself when the pressure's on," Marty said. "And who gets left alone to do what they please?"

"The 5%," Bubba said. He remembered Jimmy's remarks at the Palace: ". . . if you screw up enough, they'll quit messing with you."

"But good employees get a higher increase at their review, and they get the promotions," Bubba objected.

"That's true to a point," Marty said. "But let's look at pay and rewards."

"The 5% make close to the same money. And money can't be what's important to them, or they'd be at work more. And as for promotions . . . when was the last promotion here?"

> Pay and rewards.

Bubba thought. "I guess when Sonny got to be press supervisor," he said, "and probably mine before that."

"And that's been two years," Marty added, "so promotions aren't that frequent. So, to my last point, who gets the lion's share of . . . ?"

". . . time and attention?" Bubba filled in. "The 5%, right? I see what you mean, Marty. But you're a good guy. The other managers are OK. It ain't your fault. The 5% just stir up trouble. That's just the way it is. My brother Junior says it's the same at his place, too."

> Attention and recognition.

"I appreciate your saying that it's not my fault, but *it is the system's fault*. And I'm part of the system that puts consequences on the backs of people who are doing their best, while the 5% gets away with it. *We have to change the system to put the consequences in the right place*," Marty said firmly.

PURSUING CHANGE

- Consequences influence behavior.
- Do the consequences for high performance make sense?

For your to-do list:

❑ Make time to talk with your top performers. Tell them you appreciate what they do. Be specific. Ask them what they get for their efforts. Build the relationship with them.

A Curve in the Road

Change, for people and companies, is a process that begins with seeing the problem and understanding the consequences.

*****

"Change is tough to start, and tough to keep up." —Bubba

8

Bubba crashed through the swinging doors of the Emergency Room and stopped, sweeping the room with his eyes to find someone he could question.

"Over here, Hon!" His eyes followed the sound, spotting his wife Dottie who worked as an aide at the hospital.

Bubba walked briskly around the desk over to a curtained cubicle. Dottie stood beside a doctor just outside the cubicle.

"How is he?" Bubba asked in a loud whisper.

"He'll be all right. Fractured forearm, separated shoulder, bruised ribs," Dottie said as she embraced Bubba. "He was lucky. Real lucky this time."

The doctor extended his hand. "Hello, Bubba. Dottie

was working here in the ER when they brought him in," he said. "He's looking better."

"Can I talk to him now?" Bubba asked.

"I suppose," said the doctor. "He's alert, but may be in some pain until the medicine takes effect."

"Bubba." Dottie gripped his sleeve, pulled him aside and said quietly, "Junior's blood alcohol was .15. The deputy said drinking caused the wreck. He hit the ditch and flipped; barely missed a tree."

Bubba nodded silently. "It's not the first time," he thought as he squeezed her hand and slipped through the curtain.

Junior sat shirtless on the table in a semi-upright position, talking with a female attendant. His left shoulder, arm, and side were raw and blue, with a clean white cast on his forearm suspended from a sling. Not bad, considering.

"Hey, Junior," Bubba interrupted. "Glad to see you're well enough to flirt."

"I guess it just wasn't my time to go, huh?"

"Not this time, I reckon," said Bubba sternly, "but what about next time?" Lowering his voice, he added, "Junior, how much had you been drinkin'?"

"You ain't gonna start on me about that again, are you?" Junior whined. "I stopped by after work at The Palace, just like you do."

"Yeah, and I know Roy wouldn't let anybody get in such a shape they couldn't drive. Do you know what your blood alcohol level was? You had a .15! Are you telling me you only had a beer at The Palace?"

"Well, I stopped at the store and got a 12-pack and some

cigarettes," Junior said. "I might have had one or two more. Look, I ain't no alcoholic. All I drink is beer. A few beers ain't ever hurt nobody."

"They nearly killed you!" Bubba said.

"I ain't hurtin' nobody but myself," Junior shot back.

"Tell that to the folks at the plant that wanted you to be steward," said Bubba, "and to Carol and the kids. They only left 'cause of your screamin' and cussin' after you'd been drinking."

"I never hurt nobody!" Junior screamed.

"Not with your hands! They were just scared you were going to tear the place up and leave them with nothin'! Or show up at work drunk and lose your job. Or maybe just kill your fool self, like you almost did tonight," Bubba said in a muffled, trying-not-to-scream-in-public whisper.

Junior just glared.

"And I'm scared of losing you, too," Bubba said more softly. "Junior, why can't you see what this is doing to you? What's it going to take to make you change?"

"It ain't nobody's business but mine," said Junior. "I can do what I want, when I want, and I can stop drinking when I want. Maybe I made a mistake. I had an accident, all right? I don't need to change nothing—'cept my underwear." Junior laughed, then grimaced at the pain.

For once, Bubba didn't laugh at a wisecrack so typical of the good nature that made Junior popular. "Why can't he see?" Bubba thought. "Why's it so hard to change?"

> Change is a process, not an event—for individuals and organizations.

9

Work went smoothly the next morning. Bubba had finished the changeover on Press 4 without a hitch. He even had time to unbox and shelve the replacement parts he'd ordered. "Yep," he thought as he got his tools out for the die change on Press 8, "maybe a little too smooth."

"What's different?" he brooded. "It seems like I've had time to do everything right on schedule—like there's something missing."

"That's it," he said aloud. "Missy! She ain't called me in two days!"

"You talking to yourself, Bubba?" said Wayne.

"Oh, I reckon he misses his girlfriend," teased Sam.

"I wonder what's up with her? Is she out? Maybe she quit," Bubba thought, a bit hopefully before his conscience smacked him. "Naw—I'd have heard that by now."

A changed Missy

There she was. No sign of scrap parts. Finished parts falling into the bin in a steady, regular rhythm—the beat of a properly running, productive operator. Between cycles, she picked up finished parts, efficiently examined them under the light, and placed them in stacks.

This was Missy? Our Missy?

The break buzzer sounded and she secured her machine, then noticed Bubba standing a little open-mouthed on the perimeter. "Hey, Bubba!" She walked over. "Wanna go on break?"

"Uh, I reckon," he said. "You ain't called me today, or yesterday. Are you sure them parts are good?"

"Yep," she said proudly. "I've made production the past two days, and a good bit more. Everything's fine."

"But," he persisted., "usually, you uh . . . have a lot of . . . trouble."

> **AWARENESS**
> Seeing the need is the first step toward change.

"You mean, I'm usually a pain, right?" she said with surprising candor. Her voice dropped, almost apologetic. "I know. I have been."

They walked into the break room, and as they were sitting down, Bubba asked, "It ain't none of my business, but what made things different the past two days?"

"I got to thinking," she said, looking around at no one in particular. "My mama got laid off over at Tex-Made. You heard they were closing?"

"Yeah. Sorry. I didn't know your mama worked there."

"Well, I watched her over the weekend. I saw how upset she was. She was saying how there was so many of the workers that, well, didn't give a damn. Laying out, or causin' machines to break down so they could stand around. She said if more of them had done their jobs, maybe they wouldn't have closed," Missy said. "And I know she's worried about how she'll pay the insurance now. There ain't many hiring except the burger places, and she can't do heavy work anymore.

"And looking at her, Bubba, I realized that I was one of them—the one's she was talking about that wouldn't half work. I saw what a good job meant to her; how much it hurt

> **UNDERSTANDING**
> Why it's important; the consequences of changing and of staying the same.

her to lose it. I know I need to help her now, and my brother. And, you know, this place ain't great, but Sonny and Marty ain't too hard to work for, the people are nice, and the benefits ain't too bad. So I decided I was gonna do what I could to keep this place going."

Bubba was stunned. "So, it took you seeing what happened to her to realize you needed to change? But—no offense—you knew you should have changed before, didn't you?"

"I guess I knew what I was doin' wasn't right, but I didn't really understand why I should change before. I didn't see what was in it for me. Maybe that's selfish, but I really couldn't see it. You know, that old song's right, 'You don't know what you got 'till it's gone.' Well, maybe I got smart in time to do something." She paused. "How's Junior? I heard about the wreck."

"I reckon he'll live awhile longer," Bubba tried to joke lamely, but even he didn't find it funny.

Missy's concern was genuine. "You remember me and him dated for awhile until he started drinking a lot. Mama didn't think I should keep going with him. He's a nice guy. When's he going to stop drinking so much?"

"Well, I guess he hasn't seen what's in it for him yet, like you said," he said.

"I'm worried about him, Bubba. Should I call? I don't want him to think, you know, the wrong way, but he's got to change or he won't make it," she said.

"I wish Junior would start worrying about himself," Bubba thought.

Then Bubba encouraged Missy, "Go ahead. See if you can get through to him."

10

"These numbers have to be wrong, Sonny," Marty insisted. "We've never been that close to production on 2108s. Are you sure they're actually in the warehouse?"

Sonny nodded. "Three skids of 'em, right where they're supposed to be. Hey, Bubba, you makin' those 2108s at home and bringing 'em in?"

Bubba took Sonny's call as an invitation to the impromptu production meeting. "Naw. That's the part runnin' on Missy's machine. She's caught up, and movin' ahead."

Marty was skeptical. "Sonny, have you inspected those parts? I don't want any returns because she's not paying attention."

Before Sonny could reassure him, Bubba broke in. "Marty, just relax. Your inventory's right, and the parts are on spec. Missy's just changed her way of looking at work."

"Yeah, that's all she's ever done—look at it," quipped Sonny, his eyes narrowing. "You been helpin' her?"

"No," said Bubba, "and I can see why you don't believe it. But look at the results. She's been above production every day this week; she's at her machine on time, including after breaks and lunch; her work area's clean as mama's kitchen. She ain't called me all week, and she's running the new stock without a problem—or a complaint."

"It's got to be a miracle. Did she join a cult or something?" Sonny asked.

"Now, don't make fun of her," Marty said. "Bubba, what did happen?"

"You might say she made a commitment. She said she appreciates her job more since her mama's been laid off at

Tex-Made, and she decided to do what she could to keep it," Bubba said. "One thing's for certain: It ain't nothing we did. It had to come from her."

> **COMMITMENT**
> The third step in the change process comes from within. Ask people to commit to better performance.

"Yeah, a commitment has to come from inside," said Marty, "but why change now? We haven't threatened her job."

"Didn't have to. She finally understood what was in it for her," Bubba said. "It hadn't ever been important until she saw her mama's situation. She saw where her path might be headin', I guess, and decided she'd better get on another path. Hey, y'all ought to stop by and tell her how good she's doin'. It's awful hard to change when you been doing it the same way for years."

"Are you kiddin'? She might start screwing up again if we say anything," said Sonny.

"And that's why more people around here don't want to change," Bubba thought.

11

"Well, here come Slick and Slack now," Sonny quipped to Marty as Jimmy and Chuck rounded the corner from the break room—10 minutes late.

"Late again," said Marty.

"Jimmy!" Sonny called, "could you come here a minute?" Marty was a little surprised that Sonny would say anything to Jimmy. He decided that he'd just stand back and watch the discussion unfold.

"Your time's my time, Boss-Man. What's the problem?" Jimmy said, knowing that anything Sonny might want to talk with him about was a problem.

"There's so many; where do I start?" Sonny thought. Then, replying to Jimmy aloud, asked, "Uh, ain't you a little late getting back from break?"

"No. About the same time I usually get back," Jimmy replied.

"Oh. Well, everybody else was back 10 minutes ago."

"But Chuck and me were a few minutes late starting, cause we finished packing the order for the shipment at noon, like you said."

"Oh. So, how long were you on break?"

"About 10 minutes, like the handbook says."

"Well, if you were a couple o' minutes late getting started, and only took a 10 minute break, how could you be 10 minutes late getting back?" Sonny's voice was perceptibly higher as his throat tightened.

"Oh, we took our 10 minutes in the break room, but then we went to the bathroom and we picked up some supplies on the way back," said Jimmy. "10 minutes is what we're supposed to get, ain't it?"

"Yeah, but . . . well, you should'a been back on time. You need to make more of a commitment to your job, like everybody else," Sonny said.

"But we only were on break for 10 minutes, boss. How could we be late?" Jimmy smiled, sensing Sonny's imminent meltdown. "Listen, I got to get back to work. Chuck's way behind, and we can't miss that truck."

"Go on. But just be back on time from now on," Sonny lamely offered with a twist of artificial management authority at the end.

Think before you speak

Sonny knew he hadn't accomplished anything with Jimmy. Jimmy wasn't committed. He was obviously aware he was late, and it just didn't bother him.

Sonny turned to Marty. "Why can't I get through to him?"

"Well, one, he doesn't see the need to change," Marty replied. "And two, did you really know what you wanted to accomplish when you called him over?"

"What do you mean?" said Sonny.

"You wanted him to improve; to be committed. But had you planned what you wanted to say to Jimmy, and what you wanted him to do about it?"

"I guess I really didn't," Sonny said. "I just saw the situation and wanted to deal with it."

> **ACTION PLAN**
> Commitment without a plan is just good intentions: You need specific goals and a timeline.

"How long did you think about what you wanted to say before you started?" Marty asked.

Sonny laughed. "Oh, about as long as it took him to get from the corner to here."

The game

"Exactly how many times has Jimmy been late?" asked Marty?

"More than I can count. But I've done tried everything I know how," Sonny said defensively.

"I'm not blaming you," Marty said. "I know it's frustrating, but my point is, he's been planning what he's going to say longer than you have. You just got run over."

"Is that what this is: a game of 'chicken?'" Sonny asked.

"To Jimmy, maybe it is. He's operating by the letter of the law," Marty said.

"So, 'What's in it for Jimmy?' means 'How can I beat Sonny using his own rules?'"

"To a point, that's right. He's not asking what he should do. He's asking 'What's the least I have to do?' That's what our rules tell him: the least he can get by with. He's just playing the rules against you," Marty said.

"And since he hasn't seen any reason to change anything, talking to him or telling him off isn't really doing any good, is it?" Sonny observed.

Marty shook his head. "He doesn't understand what's in it for him yet. What's worse, everybody can see what he's doing. They see him getting by, and it discourages them."

They realized this would take more than a casual conversation, or even a good chewing out—it would take a *plan*. Missy seemed to change when she finally understood the importance to her. Maybe Jimmy never would, but if there were any hope, it would come through understanding, too. He had to see that there were consequences in not changing.

12

Later that day, Bubba walked past Missy's machine. Her movements weren't quite as crisp as before. A small scrap pile had started, with parts on the floor. She put a part directly from the machine onto the finished stack without even glancing at it.

"Hey, girl," Bubba said. "Everything going OK?"

"Yeah, fine, Bubba," she said.

"You sure?" he said, trying to brighten the gloom. "You know, I was really impressed with what you said this morning. Not many folks are willing to admit they've been wrong and do something about it. I was right proud to see the work you put into doin' better."

Missy smiled. "You're nice to say that. You've been awful good to put up with me before. I just wish somebody else would notice."

Change takes reinforcement

"Have you seen Sonny lately?" Bubba asked Missy, hoping Sonny had stopped by after Bubba's suggestion that he compliment Missy on here new work habits. "I was lookin' for him."

"Yeah. I saw him awhile ago when he was counting my finished goods. I said, 'Pretty good production for me, ain't it?' and he looked at me and said, 'It's about time you was doing what we pay you for.'" Missy paused and looked at Bubba. "I know I wasn't much good before, but can't I get a little credit for tryin'?"

Bubba excused himself with a wave and strode off. He had something to say to Sonny.

Just behind the packing area, Bubba found Sonny and Marty sorting through boxes Chuck and Jimmy had packed wrong. The Lose Brothers were leaning against the wall absent-mindedly, watching the managers with their heads in the boxes comparing parts to packing lists. Bubba ignored Jimmy and Chuck's greetings and thrust his head into the large box.

"Sonny, I'm ashamed of you!" Bubba boomed at point-blank range inside the box. Sonny and Marty's heads bobbed

up like birds on a lake.
"Don't do that, Bubba! Scare a fella half to death!" Marty gasped. "What are you so ticked about?" Sonny barked.

> "When people change in the direction you want, reinforce them."
> —Ken Blanchard, *The One Minute Manager*

Jimmy and Chuck perked up. This was about to get interesting. Marty noticed the audience and said to them, "Hey, you guys have some re-packs to do, don't you?" They slunk over to the pile of parts. Marty then walked a short distance away, signaling with eye contact for Bubba and Sonny to follow.

"Sonny, I know you ain't convinced that Missy has really changed, but she was real disappointed when you told her, 'It's about time you was doin' what we pay you for.' Nobody in management's even noticed she's trying," Bubba said quietly.

"I ain't got time to hold her hand, Bubba, and you don't either," Sonny said defiantly. "If she gets consistent, I'll say something to her at her review. But people don't deserve a medal for just doing their job a few days in a row. Think about Sam and Henry that's been workin' all along."

"But if we don't encourage her now, she won't ever be consistent. She's already starting her old habits. She's not bad yet, but not as good as she was when I first talked to her."

"See; I told you it wouldn't last," Sonny addressed Marty.

"Maybe not. But Bubba's right; she didn't deserve to be talked to like that. If we don't support her effort, she won't stick with it," Marty said. "And

SUPPORT
Resources and encouragement reinforce change.

Teach Employees to Become Their Own Coaches
by Ken Blanchard

The most important part of being an effective manager is not what happens when you are there, but what happens when you are not there! Today's managers need to be more like teachers.

Effective teachers enable the learner to move from dependency on the instructor to independence and self-monitoring.

Helping employees to improve requires praising. When an employee does something right, it's essential that a manager notice and praise the individual—even if what was done was not perfect. Praise progress or something—anything—that is praiseworthy.

Then, if improvement is still possible, a good manager will move to redirection. When someone is learning a new task or behavior, it is appropriate to redirect and give that person more information that will further improve performance.

To create a self-managed employee, the manager must teach the employee to walk through the four teaching steps alone. Employees can monitor their own performance by:

- deciding what to do;
- doing it;
- evaluating what was done; and then
- praising whatever is praiseworthy or redirecting future efforts.

I should have said something, too. How long would you keep improving if people talked like that to you?"

Sonny didn't answer.

"I'll go over this afternoon," Marty said to Sonny, "and you need to find the right opportunity to at least tell her you've noticed."

"If you both go over there falling all over her, she'll know I said something," Bubba objected.

"Then we just need to be honest, tell her we should have said something earlier but we didn't, and that we appreciate the good work," Marty said. "The truth usually works."

"Yeah, but make sure you notice exactly what she did," said Bubba. "Don't just throw out some half-baked compliment. Really look at her area, her parts, the way she organizes the material, her being on time—pick something that's really better. Something she's bound to be proud of."

"But won't it make her embarrassed or make her feel worse about the way she was?" Sonny asked.

"Not if you mean it," Marty said firmly. "And if you don't, don't bother. Now, go give our friends over there a clue net," he nodded toward Jimmy and Chuck, "and come by to see me when you're done."

Sonny walked back to lend Jimmy and Chuck an undeserved hand.

Other support

"Change is tough," Bubba said. "Tough to start, and tough to keep up."

"Yeah. I think we make it hard to give your best. And I'm wondering what other support we need to give people," Marty mused.

"Whatcha mean?" said Bubba.

"Well, like our policies. Do they really support people who try their best, or just give folks like Jimmy some more chips for their games? And the way our managers deal with people. Sonny's a good guy, but he's frustrated having to deal with the 5%. I wonder what support I need to give him to get results, you know?"

Marty was onto something. The next step would be interesting. "I need to finish the setup on 13. See ya," Bubba waved.

PURSUING CHANGE

- Change is a process, not an event—both for individuals and organizations.
- Five stages must be completed to create lasting change:
  - Awareness
  - Understanding
  - Commitment
  - Plan for Action
  - Support
- Everyone tunes in to radio station "WII-FM" (What's in it for me!).
- Awareness plus Understanding create "WIIFM."
- Commitment without a plan is just good intentions. Set specific goals with timelines.

Redesigning the System

Traditional systems rely on rules that specify the worst we'll tolerate. Effective workplaces set expectations and develop accountability by involving the 95%.

* * * * *

"Lots of folks want to make things better. They're just waitin' for bosses to listen." —Bubba

13

". . . so, you see, I'm convinced that part of our problem is that our policies and rules really tell folks how much misbehavior we'll tolerate," said Marty. "And we end up so frustrated that we really don't deal with problems. We just fuss and cuss, and hope they'll get better or quit."

Marty paused and looked at Marilyn, Specialty Products' Human Resources field representative from Headquarters. Mostly, she dealt with benefit problems, an occasional retirement, and a good deal of recruiting to fill vacancies. Pretty routine stuff, normally. This—well, this was about strategy, about philosophy, about change.

Start with expectations

Marilyn was keeping her own counsel as she took notes studiously. After all, she thought, this is a pretty good plant. Marty's proactive. Production is improving.

Attendance had always been a problem . . . and always would be. They had some turnover, but with the kind of people you hire today, that's understandable. This is no worse than other plants. That's what puzzled her about Marty's new drive. Why now?

"So," Marilyn finally lobbed to Marty, "what do you suggest we do?"

"I was hoping you might have some ideas," Marty replied. "I figured the first step might be to decide what we really expect of our people, their performance, their attendance, and so on."

"But don't people know that already?" Marilyn asked. "We tell them when to get here, when to go on break, when to come back, where to stand—they know what's expected."

"Two problems I see with that," said Marty. "One: We shouldn't have to tell people where to stand, what to think, when to do every little thing if we have high expectations and treat people like adults. Two: Our policies actually communicate something different than our real expectations in some cases."

"So you want to change policies?" Marilyn offered. This was something concrete she could deal with.

"Maybe, but there's more," Marty responded intensely. "Don't you see? We can change policies all we want, and it won't solve anything. We have to set expectations and develop accountabilities. The policies just support our expectations.

> Policies should support high expectations.

We have to set them and communicate them—ask people to make and keep commitments."

"Look, Marty, I really want to help, and I can see you're really passionate about it. If you want to change policies, we'll have to get corporate approval. It won't be easy. My advice is, if you see something else that needs to be done—defining expectations, talking with your people or whatever—just do it. But first you need to clearly identify what's wrong."

"You mean, identify the negatives; those things that really hold our good people back?"

> Identify negatives that frustrate the 95%.

"Yeah, I guess so. Where's the biggest hurt?" said Marilyn.

"That's easy: Attendance," Marty said. "Every week, one of our 95%-ers will complain to me about a 5%-er's absences."

Marilyn sank back into her chair. "It's hopeless!" she said. "We've tried point systems, no-fault systems, point*less* systems. Nothing works."

"Nothing we've *tried* works," corrected Marty. "What did all those systems have in common? We told people how much they could get away with before they were in trouble. And guess what? They lived *down* to those expectations.

"What we need is a fresh approach; one that says, 'We expect you to be here every day, on time, and we'll deal with abuses right away.' After all, Marilyn, how many of our people have a real, habitual attendance problem?"

"I don't know, but that would be easy to find," she said. "I can get Payroll to plot absences by employee for the last year. Tardies and early outs, too."

> Measure your baselines.

"My guess is, it's a handful of people with a serious pattern of problems, year after year. Their behavior leads others to believe it doesn't matter as long as you're inside the lines. The expectation becomes confused."

Marilyn began hesitantly. "Listen, Marty, I can work on the data . . ."

". . . and I can work on drafting a new expectation," Marty interjected.

". . . but you still have to figure out how to communicate that expectation. Especially how to ask people to commit to it," she concluded.

"We have to get them to see the consequences, like Bubba said," Marty muttered. "Not just what we expect, but why it's important to us and to them. It's how we approach it."

"Improving attendance won't be easy," Marilyn resumed, "You might want to consider some other negatives to tackle first."

"Yeah, I suppose you're right. I've started my list already. There are plenty of little things that irritate people because they communicate 'We don't trust you.' We don't have to say it in words; our actions give it away."

> Plan the important changes, but start small.

"Marty, aren't you afraid of losing control and making things worse?" Marilyn asked.

"Maybe, but think about it. Sure, a new approach may cause some pain, but how much hidden pain does our current approach cause? Turnover, morale, lost production, increased benefit costs, bad quality, scrap, you name it," he replied. "I don't know all the *how* yet, but I think I see the *what* and definitely the *why*."

"Hey, if a few changes can improve things, I'm behind you," she said. "Way, way behind you," she thought.

14

A few days later, anyone walking by the window in Marty's office would think that Sonny had flipped. He was gesturing forcefully as he paced back and forth in front of Marty's desk, his mouth flapping with his face pointed downward, eyes wide.

"How do you expect me to control production with an idea like this?" Sonny asked in amazement. "I can't keep some folks on the job now. With this, I'll have no idea who's supposed to be where!"

"You don't have to know," said Marty, calmly watching the production supervisor, "because the people know. Let me ask you: Have you had people coming back late from breaks and lunch before?"

"Of course I have," Sonny flapped, still pacing.

"So, if we tell people we expect them to take a 10-minute break sometime during the first and last half of their shift, and a 30-minute lunch at mid-shift, and eliminate the buzzer, do you think most people will be late? Or will it be the same ones?"

Sonny stopped in his tracks. He had to think about that. "Well, probably the same ones as now."

"And what does this practice say to the ones who are always back on time?" Marty asked.

"I guess that we expect

> Seek buy-in, explain reasons; but don't wait for total agreement.

them to do what they've always done: Be there on time to do a job."

"And that we trust them to do that job, like they always have. It's a little thing, but little things mean a lot when you're trying to change. Things like cleaning the break room, and painting the bathroom. I want to get some folks working on that after lunch," Marty said. "Let's go." Marty strode out his office door, Sonny right behind.

"And Sonny," Marty added as they walked, "what do you think about eliminating the requirement to work the day before and day after a holiday to get paid for the holiday? It's the same principle: Only a few people abuse it, and if we communicate it right, we can gain a lot of trust with the people who'd be here anyway . . ."

"Oh, no, not another change," thought Sonny.

15

"Marty," came a soft voice from the hallway outside Marty's office.

"Oh, come in, Missy. What's up?"

"I just wanted to tell you that several of us was talkin', and we think it's a good idea, lettin' us decide our own breaks. And, well, we appreciate what you said about the majority of us have proved we're responsible, and you expect us to keep that up. That means something."

Respect builds trust

"Thanks, Missy," Marty said, "but you know, it wasn't exactly a great stride for humanity. Lots of other companies let employees decide their own break times. I figure if you're old enough to work, you can tell time. It won't hurt production, since we shut down each machine anyway at break. Might even help it a little. And, we do expect everybody to take only 10 minutes, and we'll deal with those that don't. So, I appreciate the kind words, but I'm not sure I really deserve 'em."

"I ain't sure you do either," she laughed, "but it's not just that. Seems like you're trying to think about the workers a little more. Like when you come over and told me how much improvement you could see in my quality, and how important that was to you. That wasn't much, either, but I appreciated it. I figured nobody else would say nothing to you, so I decided to. 'Sides, if it was anybody but me, the others might think I was kissing up to you. See you in the morning," she waved.

"Missy, hold on a second," he called. "I'd like to ask you to think about something for me."

"OK," she said cautiously.

"I've been thinking about a different way of dealing with attendance. Some way that lets people know that we expect them here every day, on time, giving their best efforts. And that if they have good attendance regularly, they won't be in trouble if they miss a day, but if they have a pattern of missing work, they might be."

"Yeah," she said warily, "and what exactly do you want me to do?"

"I just can't get the details down on paper as clearly as I'd like. I was thinking about asking a small group to take a look at it and recommend to me what the policy should be."

| Leaders set the direction and involve people. |

"Marty, I don't know

nothin' about writing policies," Missy objected, "and I ain't sure I want to be on your team; no offense. I might catch a lot of grief on the floor."

"Yeah, but you'd also be helping us turn a major corner. Attendance is a big problem for us. And I'd want several different points of view on the team. Sonny, for example. Bubba, maybe. Somebody like Chuck or Barb who've had some . . .ah . . .," he hesitated, ". . . experience with our current system. Four to six people. It can't be just 'my team.' It's important to all of us."

"Can I let you know tomorrow?" said Missy.

"Sure. See you then."

16

Returning to light duty had been good for Junior. His friends at work were glad to have him back. Dottie had been kind enough to bring dinner to his trailer several times since the wreck.

"Dottie, could you hand me a beer while you're puttin' the food out?" Junior asked.

"No. I'll fix you a glass of tea."

He started to complain, but thought better of insulting his meal ticket.

"You aren't drinking while you're taking your medicine, are you?" she interrogated.

Caustically, he quipped, "Even I know better than that."

"Junior!"

"I'm sorry. I just get tired of hearing about my 'drinkin' problem.'"

Dottie came over and sat on the couch across from Junior's threadbare easy chair. The place was filthy, decorated in old beer cans and dusty furniture. A picture of Junior's kids hung over the fireplace. Other snapshots of their family when Carol was around were scattered on the wall. A chilling wave of sadness passed through the room.

"I'm sure you do, Junior," she said, "but face it: You *do* have a problem. You drink too much sometimes. That doesn't make you a bad person."

"It don't?" he replied doubtfully. "Then why do I feel so bad about . . . everything?"

"Because some of your actions had bad results. You and Carol split up because of your drinking. That hurts," she said. "You had a wreck, messed up your arm and your car because of drinking. Your drinking's getting awful expensive. But you're not a 'problem person,' you're a person with a problem."

"What's the difference, Dottie?" he shot back. "I'm still screwed up, ain't I?"

> To create change, focus on specific behaviors.

"The difference is, problems can be solved," she said firmly. "We're talking about behaviors—things you say or do—and those can be changed if you'll take action, get some help. Your feelings about yourself, your attitudes toward yourself and others—those will take longer. But you can start changing behaviors right now."

"Why should I?" Junior whined. "Carol ain't comin' back; she's married again. The kids are almost grown. I'm middle-aged, broke, laid up, and livin' in a dump. What's the point?"

A soft rap came at the screen door, echoed by loud bangs as the rickety metal door hit its facing. "Junior? Dottie, is that your car? Are y'all eatin' supper?"

"Think about it. You can change your behavior. All it takes is for you to make the effort," said Dottie, rising to let Missy in. "A lot of people will be there for you, Junior. It's worth it."

GREAT EXPECTATIONS

- Define what you want to be different.
- Start with negatives that frustrate the 95%. Plan big but start small.

For your to-do list:

❑ Make sure policies support high expectations.

❑ Identify the biggest negative for your 95%.

❑ Measure your baselines: productivity, quality, attendance, delivery.

❑ Identify some smaller but quick-to-solve negatives. What can you do now?

Great Expectations

Leaders have to set the direction and ask for buy-in from their people.

* * * * *

"*Workers are people, too. They'd like to be proud of where they spend most of their time.*" —Bubba

17

" . . . so I thought I'd start out our team meeting by asking each of you what your expectations are from this work we're doing on attendance," Marty said.

"That's easy," said Chuck flippantly. "I expect to get paid to sit here and yap for an hour. Then you'll do just what you want to anyway."

"Well, I expect us to think of some way to get some folks who can't get to work on time out the door," said Bubba, glaring at Chuck.

"Yeah; come on, Chuck," said Henry. "The least you can do is take this halfway serious. With folks absent, it really puts a load on the rest of us. We need to do something."

The work group on attendance hadn't started out exactly like Marty planned—it seemed there were some mixed feelings about the subject.

"I just don't see why we have to talk about it. They ain't gonna change the policy, and what we got's just fine," said Chuck. "Everybody knows what's expected."

Clarify expectations

"OK, Chuck, what is our expectation on attendance?" Marty quizzed.

Chuck paused a second, "Not to get no more points than the policy allows. Ain't it?"

"I think that's right on the money; that's what our current practice says," said Marty. "But, guys, is that working?"

"Well, it's fair I reckon," said Missy, "cause everybody gets treated the same."

"I don't know, Missy," said Henry. "First, I don't think everybody really gets treated the same. And second, even if they were, 'the same' ain't necessarily fair."

> "To treat everybody fairly, you have to treat everybody differently."
> —Ken Blanchard, *The One Minute Manager*

"How'd you mean, Henry?" asked Missy.

"Don't you see some folks who miss a lot—and keep on missing—and nothing ever gets done?" he replied.

"I talk to everybody who's over the limit," objected Sonny.

"And get 'em to do what exactly? I'll tell you what: nothing. And that's what changes—nothing!"

"Wait a minute, guys," said Marty, writing furiously on a flipchart. "We're actually making progress. First, we're identifying what's wrong with our current system. Chuck says it's OK now, and Missy says the current system is equal. Henry said he thinks it's unfair to the people who are here all the time. It treats every situation alike. And there's no change in behavior."

> Overcome obstacles through two-way communication.

Define specific behaviors

"What's this about behaviors, anyway?" said Bubba.

"Well, attendance is a behavior—something tangible a person does that you can see or hear. How can you tell if someone has met the attendance expectation?"

"You'd see 'em here!" Bubba replied.

"How often would you see them here?" said Marty.

"Well, every day."

"Even on Sunday?"

"Of course not—but every day they're scheduled to be here," Bubba said.

"So the expectation for attendance really should be 'Here every day, as scheduled.' That's a behavior you can describe, see, and track. Are they or aren't they? Yes or no? Now, when should they be here?"

"On time," said Henry, glaring at Chuck, "and that means back from lunch and breaks on time, too."

Chuck looked down at his pencil and silently mocked Henry's 'back from lunch and breaks on time, too' with lips and eyes. His hand rose slightly from the table, fingers except the middle curling slightly, preparing to flash the 'bird' but stopping before it was fully in flight. Henry continued to stare angrily.

Marty chose to ignore Chuck. "Now, explain to me what 'on time' means here. Missy?"

"I reckon it means at your work station, ready to start work. But we really can't do that, since we can't clock in no more than seven minutes before start time."

Marty hadn't thought about this contradiction. He wrote: "Conflict between clock-in and 'at workstation.'"

"So, our real expectation about attendance should be, 'Every day, on time, as scheduled', is that right?" Everyone except Chuck and Sonny nodded. "Sonny, you have a different thought?"

> Define expectations in concrete terms.

"Well, don't we need some way of measuring it? A number or something?" Sonny asked uncomfortably. "How will we know if somebody's in trouble?"

"Yeah, that's right," Chuck echoed. "We have a right to know when we'll be in trouble."

"Well, what's that number? How many days should a person miss a year?" Marty asked.

"About 12; one a month," Chuck joked. No one laughed.

"Naw, be serious," Sonny chided. "I don't know, but we need to think about it."

"OK, but we need to know how many you're going to miss if we've got to draw a line," Bubba said. "Is it reasonable that somebody could go a week without missin'?"

> What's reasonable to allow?

Henry chortled for the first time. "Not for some folks!" The rest chuckled.

"Come on, Henry. Well, Sonny, is it reasonable?" Bubba persisted.

"Sure, I think most everybody could go a week without missing, under normal circumstances," said Sonny.

"How about two weeks?"

"Yeah."

"A month?"

Sonny looked around at the others as if seeking their thoughts. "Yeah, I guess a month is pretty fair."

"How about three months?"

"Now, I don't know about that. Folks get sick sometimes. Three months without an absence can be done, but not everybody can do it."

"So then missin' four days a year should be the limit?" Bubba was obviously driving at something.

Marty jumped in. "So, if that's the line—let's make it five days—what happens when you cross it? We have to do something to you, right?" Sonny was staring, bewildered. "Can you tell me right now how many days you'll need to miss next year?"

"Well, hold on, Boss-Man," said Chuck, "That dog won't hunt. There's good and bad reasons to miss, right?"

"OK. If that's true, it's our job to agree on all of 'em," Bubba said. "Let's start the list."

Fifteen minutes later, Marty had two pages of reasons listed. Henry threw his pencil on the table and muttered an expletive.

"What's wrong, Henry?" Marty said.

> Defining behavior is harder than it looks.

"This is stupid. We've been arguin' for half an hour, and we ain't agreed on nothin'. You can't come up with a complete list of every reason somebody might need to miss work, and if you did, the jerks would just lie and use 'em anyway.*" He glared at Chuck, again.

"And that's my point," Marty said. "It's useless to define a specific point at which somebody's in trouble, or to

Empowerment Made Easy
by William Byham
author of *Zapp! The Lightning of Empowerment*

If a company wants to empower its workers, it should begin by removing stifling regulations, policies, and procedures—by asking employees what they think, listening to their answers, and acting on their suggestions. And most importantly, by giving workers increased responsibility and authority over a defined area that they can "own."

Empowerment means treating employees as "knowledgeable adults." To give workers more responsibility, mangers need more than an intellectual understanding of what needs to be done. We have identified four key empowerment behaviors that need to be taught and practiced. They are:

- maintain or enhance self-esteem
- listen and respond with empathy
- ask for help and encourage involvement
- offer help without removing responsibility for action

Training is essential, and there needs to be a variety of things included. Managers need to be taught how to encourage and support initiative, to be coaches, and to provide feedback.

list all the good and bad reasons somebody might need to miss. We can't do it in a way that's realistic and fair. Which brings us back to the expectation: 'Every day, on time, as scheduled.'"

Bubba and the others nodded. Even Chuck didn't have any objection. But Bubba had a question: "Do we really expect everybody here absolutely every day?"

"That's our expectation for any one person, but we realize that occasionally somebody may have to be out. Across the whole plant, we can't get to 'zero absences' forever, but we should still expect that you and me, as individuals, are here every day."

"So how do you get somebody to improve their attendance?" Bubba asked.

"By talking to people about expectations and commitments," Marty said.

18

"So, you and Junior seein' each other?" Bubba teased Missy after the meeting. "Dot told me you stopped by his place."

"Now, just listen here," she launched in, "I'll see who I please, when I please, and it ain't none of your business."

He laughed. "You know I'm just teasin'. I really appreciate you stopping by there."

"I was glad to," Missy said. "But that place is a wreck if ever I seen one. Looks like a cave more than a trailer."

"He just needs a little training, that's all, and a little incentive. All by himself, he hasn't seen much point in tidying up the place."

Suddenly a sort of shrill, exaggerated smacking sound interrupted: a mock kiss. They eyed each other, then looked in unison at the source of the sound: Chuck.

"What's the matter; your lips locked up on you?" Bubba asked him.

Missy came nose to nose with Chuck. "And what's that supposed to mean?"

"Well, nothing," he said, a little taken aback by her intensity, then settling into his bad-boy role. "I thought your lips might be a little chapped after kissin' up to Marty in there."

> When people attempt to change, they face pressure to revert.

"I ain't kissin' up to him or to you," she said, "but let me ask you something, Chuck. Just why do you think Marty asked us to that meeting?"

"Like I said, to flap our jaws and get out of work for awhile, so he could do what he wanted to anyway."

"Is that what you think? Let me tell you what I think, Chuck: We were there because Marty wanted to know what we thought. He's giving you credit for having a brain, not just a mouth. You, and me, and all the rest of us are here to give it our best every day so we can keep our jobs."

"I'm giving these SOBs more than they deserve," Chuck said defiantly.

"You've been listening to Jimmy too long, Chuck. I think you're better than that. And I think you can give better than you've been giving. What do you think?"

"I think you better talk to somebody who cares," he said in parting.

Missy turned to Bubba, who was too shocked to move. "I guess I shoulda just ignored him," she said. "But since I started seein' the reason I should care more about work, I just can't stand folks shootin' off their mouths like that. It's time the rest of us spoke up."

GREAT EXPECTATIONS
- Leaders set the direction and involve people.
- Build the buy-in of people who want to make things better, but don't wait for total agreement.
- 95% employees can confront 5% behavior.

For your to-do list:

❑ Ask one of your 95% employees for their ideas on solving a workplace problem—processes, logistics, equipment, workflow, etc. Or form a team to look at a specific problem and recommend solutions.

Taking It Personally

You build trust by doing what's right, one situation at a time.

* * * * *

"If you show me you care, I'll trust you. If I trust you, I'll help you." —Bubba

19

Junior swallowed hard as he walked toward the plant manager's door. He'd been there many times as steward, usually representing a fellow employee with a problem. Now it was his turn.

He tapped lightly on the secretary's door frame. "Come on in, Junior. Mike's expecting you. Can I get you some coffee?"

"No thanks, Sharon," Junior replied. His hands were a little shaky, and he didn't want to spill it on himself.

"We all really missed you while you were out. Not that we want to see too much of you now!" she joked. "He's off the phone. Go right on in."

The office seemed small and smelled of stale cigarettes. Mike stood up from behind his aging metal desk and came around it. Junior winced a little as Mike's hand raised as if to clap him heartily on his sore shoulder; then, whether aborting a joke or suddenly remembering Junior's injury, the hand dived to shake instead.

"Hey, Junior!" Mike said. "Kinda unusual to see you here by yourself, ain't it?"

"Well," Junior's voice lowered, "I got something kinda personal to talk about."

"Oh," Mike replied more seriously, quietly pushing the door shut as he motioned to a couple of side chairs, "sit down and tell me what's up?"

Mike had been a good manager since arriving two years ago. Far from being the hard-nosed, union-busting type they had expected, he really seemed to know how to work together with the union leaders. They'd had some differences, but Mike knew how to give and take. All Junior and the committee had asked was fairness, and Mike gave that. But after seeing him as an adversary—even if a friendly one—for so long, it was awkward to be here.

"I need some help, Mike," Junior said. "Since the accident, I sort of began to think."

"Yeah, that 'life passing before your eyes' stuff really happens, doesn't it?" Mike said, trying to lighten the mood.

"Well, not exactly. See, I know that . . . well, sometimes I drink too much. Never at work, now, you understand," he added quickly, "but after work. And, you know, I kinda think it's time . . . I don't know how, but . . ." Junior looked up into Mike's eyes for the first time.

"You want some help dealing with alcohol abuse, Junior?" Mike asked gently.

"Yes, sir, I do," he said. "I need some. I didn't really know who to talk to, and . . ."

"I'm glad you felt like you could talk to me about this, Junior," Mike said.

"Well, we've been through a lot together. You ain't roasted anybody that didn't deserve it yet, and I was countin' on not bein' the first one."

"Well, that's how you build trust: doing what's right, one situation at a time," Mike said. "Now, let's talk about how to get started . . . ."

20

"Getting people to be accountable; that's the key," Marty thought as he carried his tray from the serving line to the banquet room. These monthly Chamber of Commerce operations forums weren't often useful, but it did give him a chance to see other plant managers.

Active listening skills are key

As Marty sat down, the manager of the plant where Junior worked came in. "Have a seat, Mike," Marty called.

"Thanks, I will. How's things going?" Mike asked.

"Pretty well," he muttered without changing his pose.

"So, what were you thinkin' so hard about?"

Marty looked surprised, but Mike had always been insightful. That was one of the things Marty liked about him. Mike really paid attention to people, and he seemed to know what to say.

"How'd you know that I was thinking about something?"

Mike grinned. "I'd like to say it was my natural powers of perception, but it isn't. We

| Body language. |

had some training in active listening for our managers, and body language is part of that. Now, you have to be careful not to read too much between the lines, but it can sorta tell you if someone's tense, or worried, or angry or upset. You know, whether to talk or run."

"Active listening? What exactly is active about it?" Marty was clearly interested.

"Active listening is the most important skill a leader can have," Mike extolled. "See, most listening is passive. We just sit there while somebody talks. Active listening keeps both people engaged in the process by asking open-ended questions."

"What are 'open-ended questions?'" Marty asked.

> Open-ended questions.

"Open-ended questions can't be answered with a simple yes or no."

"How does that help you listen?"

"Real simple," Mike said, finishing his first bite. "It helps you get the other person talking. Gives you information that you'd miss if you were doing all the talking. Open-ended questions can only start with certain words: who, what, when, where, why, how."

"But don't people sometimes avoid answering?" Marty quizzed.

"Sure. But, you just make comfortable eye contact and wait for the answer. Resist the urge to jump in when it's quiet. Maybe use body language like nodding your head or turning an open palm to give them a cue that you're listening."

> Eye contact with silence.

"So after they answer, then what?"

> Restatement.

"Well, it depends on what they say. Many times, you restate what you heard them saying. You don't just repeat it verbatim, but summarize what their main point was. You can say, 'I want to make sure I understand,' then summarize. It checks for your understanding, and gives them a chance to add stuff."

"How do you know when people aren't telling the whole story?" Marty asked.

"You don't, but you can get an idea by watching their body language and listening to their tone of voice, their pitch and speed," Mike replied.

> Listen for total meaning.

"And, there's a place for yes or no questions, too. Like to clarify details of a story, or contradictions. 'Did you mean it happened like this, or was it like that?'"

Marty thought about Sonny and others at his plant. "This sounds tough to do. Did your supervisors really take to it, even in a union shop?"

"Yeah, and we trained the stewards, too. They need to know how to listen actively. See, most people don't like to just out-and-out lie to you, but if you don't ask the right question, they don't feel the need to volunteer much. Active listening really helps make them more accountable for their behaviors. It keeps you from having to guess at what's really going on. Plus, it builds mutual understanding of what caused the problem, and what's in it for the employee to fix it," Mike added.

Understanding before commitment

Marty thought, "I guess before you can get a commitment, both people have to understand not only what happened, but what's causing the problem. The other person has to understand why it's important, and what's expected. Active listening helps you get there. Then, you can get commitment to specific changes."

It was time for the speaker. "This guy's the one who taught our class," Mike whispered. Marty looked at the speaker's first slide to see the topic: "Active Listening Skills." "Maybe these luncheons are more useful than I thought," Marty thought.

21

"I'm gonna take you down, boy! I don't care if we both go, but I'm takin' you with me! Do you hear me?! I'm sick and tired of you thinkin' you can get by with just whatever flies into that pea brain of your'n, and they ain't a payin' me enough to put up with the likes of you. Well? What you got to say, Jimmy?"

For a moment, Marty was frozen with shock at what he heard Sonny screaming from across the pack-out room.

Things had been going pretty well, he thought. Missy had shown Barb a new way of stacking finished parts that was easier and reduced damage. The attention seemed to soften Barb a little, and she hadn't missed or been late in nearly a month. Henry had been showing the new operator next to him some techniques he'd learned, and his usually gruff veneer was peeling away to reveal his good nature. Sonny had even been seen complimenting someone for hustling to expedite an order.

Now, this. He'd heard a commotion from his office, and by the time he tracked it to the back, almost everyone had stopped to listen.

"OK, get on back to work, folks," Marty said matter-of-factly as he walked past them toward the source of the disruption. "Sonny, what's going on?" he said evenly.

Sonny loses it

"Marty," said Bubba, "It's the same thing that's been going on for as long as I can remember. This goof-off, hare-brain nitwit has mixed up part numbers, again, an' he's givin' me lip about it. I've showed him, I've helped him, I've even done it for him, but I'm tired of it and I ain't gonna put up with it no more!"

"Jimmy, I want to hear what you have to say, but I think we'd better continue this discussion in my office," Marty said, turning briskly and marching back the way he'd come. All three looked at the floor, not at anyone else, and certainly not at each other. Silence prevailed among them as Marty shut the door and pointed out seats for each.

"All right gentlemen, I'm going to ask the questions and we're going to keep this respectful, OK?" He shot Sonny a stern look. "Needless to say, I'm not real happy right now. Jimmy, tell me what happened out there."

Under the circumstances, Jimmy figured he'd keep his smart-mouth switch on "low." Innocent victim—well, victim at least—seemed to be a potential award-winning role here.

"Well, Mr. Peoples, you been talkin' about saving money on shipping by cuttin' down on partial boxes. Them parts was all going to the same customer, so I just was gonna put them all in one box. Then, Sonny come back there and grabbed the packin' list out of my hand, asked me 'What do you think you're doing?', real smart like that, and he said I was puttin' the wrong parts in the box . . . ."

"You forgot the part where you said, 'Why don't you just get off my back and let me do my freakin' job!' ain't ya?" Sonny interjected.

"Well, all I was trying to say was that I know how to do my job, and I wish somebody would trust me to do it," Jimmy replied snippily. "And I reckon with my 'pea-brain,' as you called it, I just don't know how to say it polite. I apologize," he said with enough syrup to serve the breakfast bar at the Road House. He turned his gaze from Sonny to Marty. "And after that, he just started hollerin' at me, callin' me ugly names an' threatenin' me. But you heard that yourself." Jimmy sat back smugly.

> "When you reprimand people the wrong way, they remember how badly you treated them—NOT how they misbehaved."
> —Ken Blanchard, *The One Minute Manager*

"Jimmy, we've had a long history of problems with your attendance and your performance. I want to discuss the situation with you later. I'll come get you in a little while. Go back to work, and pack the parts the way we've showed you," Marty said.

"Yes, sir," Jimmy said. He rose, made cold eye contact with Sonny, then left quietly.

"OK, Sonny, tell me what happened."

His anger defused, Sonny now realized that he was in trouble here. "The past three days, we've been getting calls from customers saying they didn't get parts that we know we shipped. They were all mixed in together so they couldn't see 'em. I talked to everybody who packs parts about it. And you know Jimmy, always trying to find the laziest way to do it. So, when I came back to check on a customer complaint about a missing order, I seen Jimmy puttin' different parts all helter-skelter in one box. So I went up and asked, 'What are you doing?' and he gave me that attitude, and I guess I lost my head."

Sonny and Jimmy are both wrong

"Sonny, what you did was to make a martyr out of Jimmy. Why did you say that?" asked Marty.

"Well, I knew that Jimmy . . ."

"No, at that point, you *assumed* that Jimmy was screwing up because of his past."

"But yesterday, I found him sittin' in the break room for half an hour. He only packed out three orders, and two of 'em were wrong. The day before, he miscounted the 6102s every single time. If they hadn't weighed out wrong, we wouldn't have caught it."

"Sonny, what did you do to address these performance problems?" Marty asked, anticipating the answer.

"Nothin' you say to him matters. He ain't ever been anything but trouble. Remember I wanted to fire him last year, but Marilyn wouldn't let me."

"I was in on that discussion, too, and I remember that we didn't have any documentation on problems other than attendance. Have you documented any disciplinary actions since then?" Sonny was silent. Marty resumed after a moment. "OK. How effective do you think you were addressing the problem this time?"

"Wait a minute!" Sonny exploded. "*He's* not doin' his job, and *I'm* in trouble? You know as well as I do that nothing matters to Jimmy. It don't matter what I do. The only thing people like him understand is a kick in the . . ."

"Sonny," Marty said sternly. "We're going to discuss this like professionals. As leaders, we have to hold ourselves to a high standard. What do you think you should have done differently?"

"Well, I should have left him alone, I guess."

Marty breathed deeply and leaned back. "No, Sonny. I'm not saying you shouldn't address problems. But you were playing 'I win, you lose' with Jimmy when you started demeaning him in public. Now, he gets to play 'You lose, I win' with you because you chose to handle it at the wrong place and in the wrong way."

The blank stare evidenced Sonny's confusion.

"Do you respect Jimmy?"

"Of course not. He ain't respectable," Sonny fired.

"And you showed that disrespect in the way you talked to him. Trouble is, everybody feels like they deserve respect, and they feel sorry for people who aren't treated respectfully. Instead of working on his behavior, you were attacking him personally. Other people don't like to see that, because they figure that sooner or later it will happen to them. So, you wanted to beat him, and instead, he beat you. You can't win by putting him down; you win by keeping control and addressing the behaviors that are a problem. What had you really planned to be the outcome of your talk with him?"

Leaders 'win' when they show respect; 'lose' when they violate dignity.

Sonny thought a minute. "I don't know. Let him know where he stood, I reckon."

Marty nodded. "Sonny," he said seriously, "do you understand what happened here?

"Yeah. The no-good, lazy . . ."

"Sonny . . ." Marty cautioned.

"Sorry. I lost my temper, and I shoulda wrote him up if he was really doing something wrong instead of hollerin' at him."

Taking a different approach

"I agree, Sonny," said Marty, "writing Jimmy up would have been a better response. I'm counting on you to do that in the future. You might want to talk it over with me before talking with Jimmy, so we can plan what we're going to do."

"Right," Sonny replied halfheartedly.

"Well, now we have to deal with Jimmy's behavior," Marty said, reaching into the drawer and removing a disciplinary action form. "What exactly did Jimmy do, and how is that different that what we expect of employees?"

Sonny thought for a moment. "Well, first off, he mixed the 6102s and the 6118s in a box, and he didn't pack 'em right."

"What exactly was wrong with the way he packed them?"

"They was jumbled up, 'stead of packed neat," Sonny replied.

"OK," Marty said as he wrote, "Part numbers 6102 and 6118 mixed in box against procedure. Used improper packing technique. What else?" he said.

"That smart comeback he made to me," Sonny replied. "He shouldn't do that, right?"

"No," Marty said as he wrote, "Disrespectful language used with supervisor." He looked Sonny in the eye. "Now, there's one more thing we have to do before we give Jimmy this disciplinary action."

> Focus on the problem behavior, not the person.

Sonny swallowed hard. "You want me to tell Jimmy I'm sorry?" Sonny said glumly, his head hanging. "I don't know if I can do it because I ain't sorry. He is."

"What do you think you need to do for everyone's benefit?" Marty said. "All I know is, if you keep playing 'win/lose' with people, eventually you get to 'lose/lose.' Nobody wants that."

Winners and Losers

As Einstein said, the definition of insanity is to do the same thing over and over and expect different results.

* * * * *

"If you always do what you've always done, you'll always get what you've always got." —Bubba

22

Jimmy shuffled his feet a bit, looking at the floor as he sat in Marty's office again. Sonny took the lead.

"First off, Jimmy, I apologize for losin' my cool out there. What you were doin' wasn't right, but the things I said was uncalled-for."

Jimmy hesitated, looking first at Sonny and then at Marty for cues as to whether the time was right for an attack. He sensed it should wait. "All right," Jimmy said noncommittally. "Is that all?" He started to rise.

"No, Jimmy, it ain't," Sonny said, irritation flashing in his eyes. Marty looked at him, wondering if he should take over. Sonny continued evenly. "The situation where I lost my temper all got started because of your performance today. Here's a disciplinary action report for you to read and sign." Sonny slid the paper across the corner of the desk. "It says that you're being wrote up because you packed parts improperly and mixed 'em up in a box, and that you was insubordinate in the way you talked to a supervisor. You got any comments?"

Jimmy pushed the paper back across the desk, sunk back in his chair and folded his arms across his chest. "No, but it ain't fair. I was just doin' what y'all said you wanted. I reckon it don't pay to think around here. I won't never pack different parts in the same box again, no matter what." There was just a hint of smirk in Jimmy's expression, leading Marty to wonder what he meant by, "no matter what."

"All right, just sign the form and we'll be done," Sonny said.

"I ain't signin' nothin', cause it ain't fair," Jimmy replied.

"Jimmy," said Marty, "signing it doesn't mean you're agreeing with us, just that you received a copy of the form."

"I know the drill, Mr. Peoples," Jimmy said, "but I still ain't signing."

"Employee refused to sign," Sonny scrawled, sliding it across to Marty. "Marty, if you'll witness that Jimmy refused to sign, we'll give him his copy. Now, Jimmy," he turned, "this is your first written warning for this offense, and like it says, if you pull anything like this again it could . . ."

". . . lead to further disciplinary action, up to and including termination, la-dee-dah," Jimmy completed sarcastically. "Yeah, like I said, I know the drill."

"Jimmy, we're giving you some consideration here," Marty replied, "and it would be in your best interests to show more cooperation. We're talking about your employment."

"Here's your copy," Sonny said, ripping the back page off the form and handing it to Jimmy. "I expect you to follow procedures in the future, and to talk more respectful."

"I reckon I will if you will," Jimmy said, rising. "Can I go back to work now?"

23

Bubba laughed as he recounted Jimmy's version of the story he'd heard in the break room.

"Yeah, Jimmy was talking just like Arnold what's-his-name in *The Terminator*. 'I'll be back,'" Bubba impersonated to Marty, and, Marilyn, here for her regular visit.

"I'm sure he will, Bubba," Marty said resignedly. "That's the problem. We can tell people what we expect in terms of performance and attendance," Marty said, "but the problem comes when someone doesn't meet the expectation. Just giving out write-ups and suspensions doesn't work, especially to people who don't seem to care. But can *anything* work?"

"Well," Bubba replied, "first off, what exactly do you want to happen when you talk with 'em about their attendance, or any kind of work problem?"

"That's kind of obvious, isn't it?" Marty said. "We want them to stop doing the wrong things, and start doing the right ones." Marilyn nodded, a bit amused at this strategy discussion between a plant manager and a set-up technician.

"Really?" said Bubba, grinning. "I thought the point was to get rid of 'em."

"Well, sometimes that happens, but we don't want it—I guess," Marty said tentatively.

Bubba chuckled. "I wouldn't be too sure. If you read the policy, it looks like you really plan to fire 'em."

Marty saw his point. Something had always made him uncomfortable with treating people worse and worse in the hope they'd behave better and better. The fear that the real intent was to fire people made supervisors avoid addressing problems until it was almost too late—or simply yell, scream, and swear instead of using the process. Like Sonny.

"And the stupid thing is, I ain't ever seen it do much good, anyway," Bubba continued. "The ones you want to fire can play the game, and the ones you ought to help just get tore up about it."

"Like Jimmy who's constantly skating on the edge, and Sam who got punished for an honest mistake," Marty thought. Specialty Products' discipline system, like most, consisted of the familiar one-page, preprinted form for write-ups, filled out before the employee came in—except, of course, for the one-inch employee comments section which they usually either left blank or filled with bad language. Took about five minutes, and the results didn't even last that long. There was almost no discussion of why the problem occurred, or any commitment to change behaviors.

Another problem was that disciplinary actions were typically for one or two specific rules violations, not for a pattern of misbehavior. That's what Jimmy had meant by saying, "I won't pack those parts together, no matter what." He intended a kind of malicious obedience, changing only the specific behavior defined on the disciplinary form.

And, of course, if the employee could avoid that specific violation for a certain length of time, he got to repeat the step the next time. No wonder the jerks called the forms "toilet paper." Still, the system was legal, and the forms provided documentation. And, frankly, he'd never heard of anything different. Marty glanced at Marilyn.

"You know what I think? We need to start over," said Marty.

"Well, what would you suggest?" Marilyn asked.

"That's the problem. I don't know what to do differently. I just know what we have doesn't work," said Marty.

"Well, when you're talking to somebody about a problem they got, what's the first thing you want to make sure of?" Marilyn asked.

Marty thought about the change process, "First, we have to make sure they're aware of the problem—what the expectation is, and how their actions differ from that."

> Make expectations crystal clear.

"Yep, you're right," Bubba said. "Most folks know what's expected, but some might not. How you gonna do that?"

"Obviously, we have to talk to them one-on-one, in private. Instead of just telling them what they have to do, we should *ask* them what they believe the expectation is, and how they believe their behavior matches up. You know, get them involved in solving the problem. Then we can clear up any misunderstandings, and get their commitment to meet the expectation," replied Marty.

> Use performance counseling to build personal accountability.

"So you'd write 'em up?" Bubba asked.

Marty thought about it—did he really believe that most people wanted to do what's right?

"No," he finally said. "I don't think so."

"But, supervisors ought to make a note that the conversation occurred, maybe on their calendar or something, even if they put nothing in the file yet," Marilyn added prudently.

> Document informal conversations.

"OK, what next?" asked Bubba.

Marty smiled and said, "Well, of course, the problem is solved!"

Marilyn snickered.

"Even if they keep on screwin' up?" Bubba asked.

"Well, you'd have to have flexibility based on the behaviors you see. Is the person trying and can't get it, or is the person obviously seeing how far he can push you? To find out what's behind the continuing problem, I think you have a second conversation," said Marty.

"Oh, so you're gonna talk 'em to death?" Bubba said.

"No. This second conversation would focus on why they didn't keep their commitments. This is much more serious than the first one because if they don't keep their commitments, you can't trust them and continue to work with them," Marty explained. "This time, you document. But our current form doesn't seem like the right way to do it."

> Find the reason behind continuing failure.

Marilyn looked around. In Marty's in-box, she could see a couple of memos from corporate. That gave her an idea. "Marty, think about it—when there's been a problem involving a couple of managers, how do they keep a record of who agreed to what?"

"A memo," Marty said, catching her train of thought, "summarizing what was said,

> Use a memo to specify problem behaviors, new behaviors expected, and the employee's commitment to change.

and who agreed to do what. Instead of a form, we should just write a summary memo after the meeting. Put in it what the employee said, and what they agreed to do. And," he added, "explaining that this can't continue without sustained improvement. You have to let them know that this is very serious, and that they could lose their job."

"So, what you're really doing at this point is recording their commitment." Marilyn said.

"More than that. We're really seeking a deeper commitment, not just clarifying the expectation like we were the first time. And documenting it, too," Marty said.

"So let's say that don't solve the problem," Bubba said. "How long do you keep a-jawin' about it?"

"Not long," said Marty. "Once a person makes a commitment, they're accountable for it. If they don't live up to it, you move forward. After the second conversation, I think you have one more chance in most cases. That's it."

> Hold people accountable for the commitments they make.

"But it would depend on the situation, wouldn't it?" asked Bubba.

"Sure. There are clearly some things employees should be fired for immediately . . ." Marilyn said.

"Such as?" Bubba asked.

"Flagrant abuses like violence, theft, sleeping on the job. Those things ordinarily bypass the early conversations and go straight to dismissal."

"But don't you need a little leeway for judgment even in those?" Bubba asked.

"You still have to listen to the person, get the facts, and talk to witnesses," said Marilyn.

"Right. Nothing should be automatic. You need flexibility to start at any phase," said Marty, "but those situations will be rare. We should expect that most problems will be solved after one conversation. Some will require two. And if there isn't lasting improvement, we should have one final attempt."

"Kind of sayin', 'We can't go on like this,'" Bubba said. "This is the point where they have to decide if they want to keep their job."

"And the company has to decide if we really have any reason to believe they'll improve," said Marty. "We ought to ask people to go home and think about it."

> Give one last chance.

"Whatcha mean, 'think'?" Bubba asked. "It wouldn't take me long to decide that."

"Yes, but legally we have to give people due process," said Marilyn. "It's not right to ask them to decide on the spot."

"And when they come back the next shift, they need to bring a plan for how they will improve their attendance, or quality, or production, or whatever it is," said Marty.

> Require a personal plan for change.

"So we can sorta see if they're takin' it serious?" Bubba said. "Yeah, I like that. But some folks can't hardly write their name, much less a plan."

"The writing's not important; the plan is," Marty said. "We can help them write it down, but they have to think it through and commit to it. Remember, Bubba, at this phase, we're at the end of the trail. We've already had at least two detailed conversations with them except in rare situations.

detailed conversations with them except in rare situations. We can help, but it has to be their commitment."

"So what if they come in and say, 'Tell me what to do, boss, and I'll do it?'" Bubba asked.

Marty shook his head. "Not good enough. We need them to take responsibility for solving the problem."

Firing with respect

"So if the problem employee don't improve after this, or if they won't come up with a plan you can believe, they're fired, right?" said Bubba.

"Yes. And we don't want to kick them while they're down. No screaming. We need to be as professional and respectful when they're leaving as when they came," said Marty.

"Maybe you should offer 'em a chance to resign," said Bubba, "to kinda preserve a little bit of dignity. After all, they're probably gonna tell their buddies that they quit, regardless."

Marilyn nodded agreement. "Yes, if it's for ongoing performance, we should let them resign. It's called a requested resignation. On the other hand, if it's for gross misconduct like theft or violence, we should not give them that option."

"Won't resigning make them ineligible for unemployment? They'll probably ask that," Marty asked.

"We don't make that determination, Marty; the state does," said Marilyn. "They have criteria to follow. We simply supply the state with accurate information about the reason for termination."

They both paused. It almost seemed too simple as Marty made notes in his daybook:

> Clarify expectations---
> First, clarify the expectations and gain agreement to improve.
>
> Develop commitment---If the problem persists, further develop the commitment and an action plan.
>
> Decision time---
> If that fails, reach a point of decision for

"Guys, can this work? If it's really this simple, why isn't everybody doing it?" Marty asked.

"I reckon some people are. You just never hear about 'em, cause their business ain't in a uproar all the time," said Bubba.

"Sure, Bubba," said Marilyn, "they expect people to do right, and for the most part they do. They don't have a lot of

> both the employee and the company.
>
> Discharge -- maintain respect and accountability. If improvement isn't maintained, part ways with dignity.
>
> Keep it flexible to start at any phase depending on the circumstances. Above all, maintain respect and accountability.

problems, because they expect people to have self-discipline."

"And they don't take 15 years to fire somebody who ain't puttin' forth the effort, either. See, they've figured out what winning really is." Bubba continued, "It ain't beating the other guy; it's beating the problems with the other guy. Respect is what winning's all about."

REDESIGNING THE SYSTEM

- Identify negatives which frustrate the 95%.
- Plan the important changes, but start small.
- Seek buy-in, explain reasons, but don't wait for total agreement.
- Leaders set the direction and involve people.
- Overcome obstacles through two-way communication using Active Listening.
- Leaders "win" when they show respect; "lose" when they violate a person's dignity.
- Use a performance counseling process to develop personal accountability.

For your to-do list:

- ❏ Examine your discipline or corrective action policy. What's its real focus: problem-solving and commitment or completing forms?
- ❏ If it needs work, think about the Change Process. How can you create awareness, understanding, and commitment among those who must approve?

Ensuring Accountability

Treating people with respect means expecting them to act like adults—and confronting problems immediately and directly.

"Seems to me if people give better, they oughta get better." —Bubba

24

Marilyn had told Marty to expect that the policy changes he wanted to make would not be warmly received. Still, he wasn't prepared for the objections he heard from Tom, corporate Vice President of Human Resources, as they talked by phone.

"I understand it's different . . . but nothing else has worked," Marty said. "Marilyn from your office thinks we should give it a chance."

"But with this approach, we'll be vulnerable to legal charges," Tom said.

"No more than we have been in the past," Marty reasoned. "The counseling process we developed will require skills training for supervisors, but it provides due process and documentation."

"But from what I can see, only after the second step," Tom retorted. "It doesn't give enough repeated warnings. And, we need to allow ourselves the option to suspend people."

"But Tom, we've been suspending people for years. The jerks see it as a vacation, and it's humiliating to the people who care. In my experience, suspensions rarely work—especially when we're suspending people because they won't come to work."

"Humph," Tom replied, obviously unable to counter the logic. "Well, how will you ensure supervisors are consistent if there is no specified line that people cross before talking to them? We'll be overrun with complaints of favoritism."

Not just "being nice"

"It's my job as manager to work with the supervisors to review attendance records and make sure that people are being dealt with fairly," said Marty. "Tom, all I'm trying to do is create a system which sets a high expectation, and then work with people to hold them accountable for their commitments. This kind of approach is new for us, but has worked at other places."

"But it's too lenient," Tom objected.

"How can it be lenient, when we don't define any certain amount of time that it's OK for people to miss?" Marty inquired. "If anything, it's less lenient. We as managers will have to record time missed and talk with people before problems become serious."

"Marty, people need to have a line; they need to know when they'll be in trouble," Tom said. Marty shook his head at the irony; this was the same comment that Chuck, a person with poor attendance, had made in the attendance team meeting. "Besides, we can't have one plant that's different from our other plants. It'll be chaos."

"But Tom, how can it be chaos for anyone but us? It's our responsibility."

"Have you talked with Frank about this?" Tom quizzed. "As Vice President, he'd have to approve this."

"Yes, I've mentioned it to Frank, and I sent him this proposal at the same time I sent it to you. He wanted to get your views. We haven't talked in detail yet."

"Well, I'll call him to discuss it. I want us to take some time and think this through before rushing into it. In the meantime, just crack down on abusers using the policy you have. I guarantee you'll get results," Tom said.

"Yeah, just as bad as always," thought Marty.

"Besides, Marty, this is really a bad time to be talking about changing anything. We're preparing for compliance audits; we have depositions in

> Change is always difficult; it's never the "right" time to change.

several cases, and major benefits changes are coming up. I don't see how we can address this before next year."

"If we're too busy to address problems, how will we ever get better?" thought Marty. He ended his conversation with Tom, "Well, let's get with Frank to see what we can work out. This is important to us. Bye."

"Who were you talkin' to so serious?" Bubba asked from the doorway, where he'd been listening.

"The VP of HR. He doesn't like the policy we drafted on

attendance or the counseling process. Says it's too risky; it won't work; it isn't consistent with the other plants; it will cause favoritism; and on and on."

"It sure is easy to find reasons not to do something, ain't it?" Bubba said.

"I wish I could figure out what his real problem is," Marty said.

"You know, I bet a lot of it's just being afraid of a different idea, or bein' comfortable with the way things have always been. Some's probably just bein' cautious, wantin' to protect the company."

> Don't waste momentum trying to argue with hard-core skeptics. Let results speak for you.

"Yeah, it's easy to see what might go wrong with a new idea. I just wish he could see what's going wrong now."

"Well, when I'm about to do something new that people say won't work, I sorta like to have a trial run; you know, test it out real good," Bubba suggested.

Marty stopped pacing. "That's a good idea, Bubba. We could be a pilot, a test case. Give us a certain amount of time; measure the before and after results, and see how it works. I'll suggest that to Frank."

Marty picked up the phone. "Now to see if my boss trusts me to get results," he thought.

25

Getting approval from Frank, Marty's immediate manager, for a pilot of the new attendance approach and counseling policy wasn't too difficult. They had agreed on a target of 96% average daily attendance within 6 months—even though Tom thought it was impossible.

"Now, to convince the employees," Marty thought as he prepared to roll it out.

Presenting the new plan

Several members of the attendance policy team spoke at the employee meeting to announce the change. Bubba went first—everyone knew him, and almost everyone appreciated his honesty. "Not everybody on our team was entirely sold on this approach, especially at first," he said. "But we did agree that we needed to do something about attendance. Our old point system and no-fault policies don't work."

For a moment, Bubba was afraid Chuck might disagree, but finally even he nodded yes. Jimmy and a couple of others stared at the floor as Missy and Henry gave the rationale for the change. Most of the employees sat with arms crossed, heads leaning slightly to one side, mild skepticism on their faces.

Marty then outlined the basics of the attendance policy. The expectation was "every day, on time, as scheduled"; there were no set number of days it was OK to miss. Doctors' notes would no longer be required. Supervisors would record attendance on special calendars that would allow them to spot patterns. Marty would meet with each supervisor monthly to review calendars and discuss any potential problems. Emphasis would be on direct, honest communication about absences. Call-in notification to the supervisor was still required.

He then moved to the counseling policy. When it looked like a problem was developing, performance counseling would be used to discuss the cause and gain commitment to a solution. He explained the four phases: *Clarifying Expectations, Seeking Commitment, Decision-Making Time,* and *Discharge.* Counseling could begin at whatever phase was appropriate based on the situation. Suspensions were eliminated, but dismissal could result if problems weren't fixed. People would be held accountable for their performance and their commitments. And finally, all current disciplinary actions for attendance—and only for attendance—would be nullified. Everyone would start with a clean slate.

"I want to emphasize that the vast majority of people will not be impacted at all by this change," Marty concluded, "because the vast majority are here every day, on time, now. People who 'walked the line' in the past will see a difference. We'll meet with each of you over the next two weeks to discuss your situation and answer any questions."

There was a general buzz as people dispersed. Jimmy began lobbying. "You know what they're doin' this for, don't you," he said to Barb and Missy as they walked toward the door. "They're gonna get rid of us that's been here a long time and bring in cheaper labor."

"How they gonna do that, Jimmy?" Missy asked.

"Easy. They're gonna fire you if you miss even one day. Didn't you hear him? 'Every day, on time.' So Barb, if your baby's sick and you take him to the doctor, you'll get your pink slip."

"They couldn't do that, could they?" Barb asked Missy.

"Don't make much sense, does it?," Missy said. "But I'll talk to Marty to make sure."

As Missy left, Jimmy said to Barb, "Yeah, she'll go talk to Marty, but you wait and see who gets it first. It won't be his pets, I'll tell you that. I ain't waiting around to let them screw us."

26

Marty and the supervisors were holding one-on-one meetings with employees to discuss the new attendance policy and expectation. Although the purpose was to give special attention to people whose historical performance suggested they might have trouble meeting the expectation, they had decided to start with a few "easy" employees. Sam was Marty's first. Marty was finding that even Sam wasn't so easy, after all.

"How do we know the company won't take advantage of us?" Sam asked. Since his suspension, he was more suspicious of company actions than before.

"But your attendance is good. I wish we had 100 like you," Marty said. "What do you mean when you say the company might 'take advantage' of you, Sam?"

"Well, suppos'n I was to get bad sick, like a heart attack," Sam said. "Wouldn't you kick me out the door?"

This sounded like Jimmy's work. In the two weeks since the meeting, Jimmy'd had his own one-on-ones with almost everyone, planting seeds of doubt about the intent and the impact of the new policy.

"I understand your concern,"Marty said. "But that would be foolish on our part, wouldn't it, Sam? Why would we want to get rid of our best people?"

"Yeah, but there ain't any guarantee, is there?" Sam said. He was upset, and afraid. "The old way, at least we knew how far we had to go. This way, it's just whatever the boss says."

"No, Sam, it isn't," Marty said. "If you're afraid of losing your job when you get sick, remember that we have a leave policy and a disability policy, too. If you were seriously ill, you'd go on leave of absence. Then if you didn't get well enough to work, you'd receive disability. That's the same as it's always been. All we've done is take away the excuses and the lines that the 5% uses to play games."

"How will I know if I'm in trouble?" Sam asked, half convinced.

"Sam, you haven't ever been in trouble for attendance. Just look at your attendance calendar. Are you planning to start missing work now?" Marty teased.

"Now, you know I don't mean it that way," Sam retorted. "I always believed that a fair day's pay deserved a fair day's work, and I ain't plannin' to change now."

"And your attendance proves your commitment, Sam," Marty said. "If you're sick, whether for a day or a long time, you won't be in trouble. Those who have a pattern of missing work will be in trouble.

> Even the 95% can fear change—so when people resist, build understanding through active listening.

The supervisors will meet with me each month and go over attendance records, to keep track of the problems and to make sure we're fair."

"So, you ain't out to fire people?" Sam asked tentatively.

"No, not unless someone's attendance pattern shows a lack of commitment to be here on time every scheduled day," Marty said. "Then we'll have to either see a change or part company with them."

ENSURE ACCOUNTABILITY

- Don't waste momentum trying to argue with hard-core skeptics. Let results speak for you.

- Even the 95% can fear change—so when people resist, build understanding through active listening.

96

Making a Difference

*Expect changes to be challenged . . . your
response communicates your commitment.*

*****

*"Don't be surprised when people
try ya."* —Bubba

27

About a week after implementation of the new attendance expectation, Chuck and Jimmy were both absent on the same day, and neither called in to report the reason for the absence.

"Reckon I'm gonna have to grab some cables and jump-start them boys,*" Sonny said to Marty. "I don't care how you handle 'em, you can't change people like that."

Marty was disappointed in Chuck—and a little surprised, since Chuck seemed to support the change. Next morning, Marty was near the employee entrance when Chuck arrived, his head hanging down. Chuck tried to blend in with the group and go straight to his work station.

"Missed you yesterday, Chuck," Marty called, then walked over as the rest of the crew went into the building. "Was anything wrong?"

Marty knew where Chuck had been. Several employees had seen Jimmy and him at The Palace the night before. Jimmy was really piling it on about Chuck's becoming "Marty's boy." He'd dared Chuck to lay out and go fishing. Apparently, Chuck had.

> Remember—it's a person with a problem not a problem person.

"No, sir," Chuck said awkwardly, his gaze still fixed on the ground. "Just a little under the weather, that's all." Marty mused that the sun on his face indicated the weather he was under must have been nice.

"What kept you from calling in?"

Chuck's eyes peeked up from under the brim of his cap. He could see that Marty wasn't angry, but maybe a little disappointed. "Uh, I just forgot, I guess." The silence seemed to Chuck to last for five minutes, though it couldn't have been more than a couple of seconds.

"Chuck, you know that when we were establishing the attendance policy, we emphasized the importance of calling in, as well as being here every day. You remember?"

Chuck nodded. Marty observed that he looked like a kid on his way to the principal's office. "Sonny's your supervisor, and he'll talk with you later today about your reason for not calling in, because that's a problem we can't ignore. But I just needed to ask you for my own satisfaction: Were you sick yesterday? Honest—just you and me."

"Marty, I've jerked you around a little, but I ain't never lied to you, and I ain't gonna start now," Chuck said. "No, I wasn't sick. I went fishin'. I didn't call in 'cause I wasn't near a telephone." Chuck's posture visibly straightened as he talked, like a weight was lifted off his back.

Stay calm and hold people accountable

"I didn't think you'd lie to me. I appreciate that, Chuck." Marty said. "You're not that kind of person. But how do you think what you did measures up to our expectation on attendance?"

> "When you have to reprimand, focus on thebehavior, not the person. And let the individual know that you're disappointed."
> —Ken Blanchard, *The One Minute Manager*

"Not good at all," Chuck said. "I shouldn't a done that. It was Jimmy's idea . . ." he halted in mid-excuse, "but I went along with it. You got my word, that's the last time I'll lay out unless I'm bad sick or something. And if I have to be out, I'll call."

"I'm counting on that. Did you catch anything?" Marty asked, smiling.

"No, that's the worst part—all I caught is grief from you!" Chuck smiled.

Sure enough, after Sonny counseled both Chuck and Jimmy on their absence and failure to call in, Chuck's attendance was outstanding. Amazingly enough, Jimmy's attendance was perfect, too, for over a month—although he was still giving the minimum on the job.

One morning a few weeks later, Bubba stuck his head into the office about 15 minutes after start-up. "Y'all seen Chuck this morning?" he asked Sonny and Marty.

"No, come to think of it, I ain't," Sonny said. "His buddy Jimmy's back there in Packin' if you need something."

Just then they heard the squeal of car tires turning too fast, then the crunch of gravel under wheels from the parking lot. Moments later, the employee door burst open and

Chuck came flying through. His shirt tail was half in and half out; his hair (which was never too neat) was sticking up randomly like a porcupine hit by lightning. He grabbed his timecard, slammed it in, and almost leapt into Marty's office. Bubba's wrinkled nose gave evidence that Chuck hadn't showered recently. All their mouths hung open, and Chuck's tongue hung out. He spoke before anyone had a chance.

"Real sorry I'm late," Chuck said breathlessly. "My clock got cut off and I woke up 15 minutes ago. I come as fast as I could."

"Slow down, man," said Sonny, "We just found out you was late."

"I gave both you and Marty my word that I wouldn't be absent or late no more 'less it was a emergency," Chuck said, "and I don't like to break my word. I'll work over tonight to make it up if y'all will let me."

"Have a seat just a minute and catch your breath before you go to work," Marty said. As Chuck breathed deeply, Marty said, "Chuck, I appreciate your effort to let us know what's going on, and I especially appreciate your honesty. You understand what our expectation is . . . ."

To deal with problem behaviors:

- Ensure awareness of the problem and understanding of its importance.
- Give them a chance to explain; listen actively and ask open-ended questions.
- Ask for their commitment to a specific change.
- Look for specific action plans that bring intent to life.
- Support good-faith tries even if they stumble.

"Yes, sir," Chuck panted, "every day, on time."

"And how do you feel that you met that expectation today?"

"Not good."

"So, how are you going to make sure that this doesn't become a pattern?"

Chuck's mouth twisted momentarily. "A pattern?"

"In other words, how you gonna keep this from happening over and over?" Sonny clarified. Marty was impressed.

"Oh, I'm gonna move the clock to where nobody can hit it by accident, tell my family not to touch it, and be sure to check it before bed," Chuck said. "I might even get me a battery clock in case the power goes out."

"Chuck, I appreciate your commitment, and we expect you to live up to it. I know you won't let this mess up the improvements you've made lately," Marty said.

28

Bubba figured trouble was brewing when he saw Jimmy hovering around Chuck right after the incident.

". . . so what'd he say then?" Jimmy quizzed.

"Well, after I told him how I was gonna make sure I was on time in the future, Marty just said he appreciated my commitment, he expected me to live up to it, and that he knew I didn't want to mess up no more," Chuck replied.

"That's it? No write up or nothin'?" Jimmy said. "Cool."

Bubba ran into Sonny later. "You might keep your eye peeled for ol' Jimmy. I heard him pesterin' Chuck about what was said to him this mornin'."

"I hope they're not plannin' some more foolishness,"

Sonny said.

"Naw, at least Chuck ain't. He told Jimmy he appreciated how you an' Marty treated him, and he wasn't gonna lie to nobody," Bubba said, "but that don't apply to Jimmy."

29

Sure enough, at starting time the next morning, Jimmy wasn't at his work station. He ambled in through the back entrance about 10 minutes late, whistling. He waved and spoke to a couple of people on his way to the time clock, punched in, and casually strolled back toward his area. Sonny intercepted him about halfway.

"Mornin' Jimmy. I noticed you was a little bit late this mornin'," Sonny said.

"Yeah, so?" Jimmy volleyed. "I ain't as late as Chuck was yesterday, and you didn't do nothin' to him. So you can't do nothin' to me."

"Jimmy, that ain't the point. You were late just now, so I'm concerned about your performance."

"Oh, but I got rights. You can't treat me no different than you treated him." Jimmy's arrogance fairly leapt from his expression.

> A performance problem exists when:
>
> - a pattern of misbehavior or poor results continues without sustained improvement
>
> - misbehavior is found to be intentional or malicious
>
> - a behavior violates laws or shows disrespect for others or the company (fighting, stealing, abusive language)

"This is about you, not about Chuck. What's your understanding of what we expect about bein' on time, Jimmy?" Sonny asked.

"You can expect what you want to. I wasn't as late as Chuck, so I'm just goin' on back to work now." He walked away. Sonny was flabbergasted.

Confront the 5%

"Jimmy!" Sonny called out as he walked to catch him, "We need to go and talk with Marty about this, right now."

"The Constitution of the U.S. of A. says I got the right to free speech, and I don't want to talk to nobody, so I ain't goin',*" Jimmy said smugly.

"Well, the Constitution says citizens can keep and bear arms, but you ain't allowed to bring guns in here, are you?" Sonny replied. "This is a place of work, and the law allows us to regulate what you do here. Right now, your assignment is to come with me to Marty's office. If you don't, that's insubordination and you'll lose your job. It's your choice. You comin' with me, or not?"

"Well, I reckon if you put it like that," Jimmy said, mostly to the folks nearby who were watching.

A few minutes later, Marty listened to Sonny's explanation of Jimmy's behavior that, under the circumstances, Marty thought was delivered pretty calmly. Looking at Jimmy, Marty said, "Jimmy, this is much more serious than tardiness. Why did you say that to Sonny?"

"Since you won't tell us how much we can be late, I'll just have to make my own rules," Jimmy said, "and I figure since Chuck was about 15 minutes late, you have to let us all be 15 minutes late."

"Jimmy, what do you understand our expectation on your attendance to be?"

"I told you, I ain't as bad as Chuck," Jimmy replied.

"That's not our expectation on attendance," Marty said. "We expect people to be here on time, every day. . ."

"But Chuck wasn't! That ain't fair!" Jimmy interrupted.

"Jimmy, let's get to the bottom line. Would it be fair to say that you don't fully agree with our expectation that people should be at work every day, on time?"

"That's right, 'cause it ain't fair."

"Understanding that you don't *fully* agree with it, are you willing to commit to meeting that expectation yourself?"

> Focus on behavior and commitment, not attitude, personality, or the past.

Jimmy stiffened. This was a new and unexpected tactic. He could lie, or he could challenge. "You can expect what you want. I expect you to be fair," Jimmy said.

Marty frowned. "Jimmy, as I said, this is very serious. We've come to a point of decision for both of us. You have to decide whether you want to work here. If you do, we need to see some lasting changes in your commitment starting immediately. Your behaviors in the areas of attendance and respect for leaders are not acceptable. We both need some time to think this through carefully. I want you to take tonight to think it over, and decide whether you want to make the commitment necessary to keep working here."

"I ain't resignin' if that's what you're gettin' at," Jimmy said.

"You don't have to, Jimmy," Marty said. "We hope you'll decide it's worth it to change, because you're an experienced person. But if you don't, we have a decision to make, too.

"Here's what I suggest you do," Marty continued. "Here's a blank sheet of paper. Take some time and write on one side all the things you like about working here. Then, on the other side, write down all the things you dislike about working here. Look it over, and see if it's worth it to change. If it is, we expect you to come up with a plan on how you will improve your performance and your commitment. We'll meet with you first thing tomorrow to go over your plan and make our decision."

"You gonna pay me overtime for doin' that?*" Jimmy shot back.

Marty paused. He could see where this path was leading, but knew he had to provide due process. "The piece of paper is a suggestion, not a requirement. However, I expect you to be prepared to make a commitment and to explain how you plan to change your behavior. You have to make a choice.

"You'll go back to work now for the rest of the day," Marty said. "What actions do you think we expect of you for the rest of today and tonight?"

> Credible consequences work—emotion doesn't.

"You want me to be a good boy," Jimmy said, smirking.

Marty ignored the sarcasm. "In essence, that's right. I understand you aren't happy with this situation, but we expect you to finish the day with acceptable productivity and behavior if you want to stay employed.

"Jimmy," Marty concluded, "I really hope you'll take this seriously, because I don't want you to lose your job, and that will be the result if you aren't prepared to commit to a plan for improvement we can accept. Then, we'll have to make a decision. See you in the morning."

After Jimmy's wordless exit, Marty turned to Sonny. "Well?" he asked.

"He's more trouble than he's worth," Sonny replied, wringing his hands, "and besides, my nerves can't take many more like him. I hope he quits."

30

Back on the floor, operators were talking about Sonny's encounter with Jimmy.

"I think his rope's about run out," Sam chimed in.

"Naw . . . Jimmy's beat worse than this before," Henry said glumly.

"He'll wriggle off the hook again," Barb pronounced with certainty as Chuck arrived to transport finished parts to the back. "What do you think, Chuck?"

Chuck just shrugged and walked away.

"Not quite hisself today, is he?" Henry said.

It was obvious that Chuck's movements were slower, his eyes downcast, his shoulders a bit stooped. He acknowledged the operators, but didn't pause to joke or chat.

Missy noticed the difference when Chuck came over to move her finished parts. He barely said hello, keeping his eyes on the task.

"Hey, Chuck, what're you so down in the mouth about?" Missy said.

"Oh, I'm OK," he replied unconvincingly.

"Come over here a minute." He obliged, and as they

made eye contact, she said, "This ain't like you, mopin' around. What's up?"

"Just thinkin' about Jimmy's all," Chuck replied.

"Yeah. I saw him raggin' on you back there yesterday," Missy said empathetically. "But Chuck, you can't let him get you down."

"Well, that didn't bother me. I guess I feel bad that he got in trouble this mornin' 'cause a what I told him. Kinda hate to go back there and face him."

"Listen here, Chuck," she said, idling her machine momentarily. "We've worked here a long time, and we both had our share of problems, ain't we?"

"Yeah, reckon we have," he said.

"Jimmy's responsible for his life. You can't control what he does. He's playin' a game that he might be about to lose, but you didn't cause his problems. Don't let what he does drag you down. Listen, buddy, I finally figured out that if this place is gonna make it, I'd better grab an oar and start pullin'. I think you're on board with me, 'cause I see you getting things picked up on time, keepin' after it all day, lookin' to help out the other operators, and cleaning the place up a little. Am I right, or is that your angelic twin brother I been seeing?"

The corner of Chuck's mouth turned up a little in a half-smile as she looked into the center of his eyes. There was a clarity there she wasn't used to.

"Yep. You're right."

"Chuck, it's a trip to see what we can do when we give ourselves a chance," Missy said.

31

"Ow!"

Marty's razor had claimed another patch of flesh as he readied for work the next morning. "Tough night," he thought, recalling his fitful anticipation of the meeting with Jimmy in an hour. "It had to be this way," he reflected on his action with Jimmy, "but will performance counseling work?" And, in his heart, he wondered what he really wanted to happen—improvement, or termination?

He wasn't sure he wanted to think about that one too long.

At work, Jimmy peeled into the parking lot at starting time on the nose. He had the clock tolerance down with mathematical precision. At one minute after starting time, he hit the door. At two after, he tossed his coat in the locker. At three after, on his way to the clock, a couple of his buddies stopped him. They looked a little concerned, but his gestures and laugh indicated 'No problem.' At five after he punched his card, then ambled for Marty's office, whistling leisurely. Nearby operators willed their machines to run more quietly as they waited for the show to begin.

Maintaining respect

Marty spotted him approaching and called, "Come in, Jimmy. We've been expecting you." In the room were Sonny and Marilyn, the personnel representative from headquarters. "This must be bigger'n I thought," Jimmy thought, uneasy because they all seemed unusually calm.

"What's up, Boss-Man?" Jimmy said. He had a toothpick between his teeth, which he pulled out as he sat down.

"Well, that's our question for you. What thoughts did you have about your behavior yesterday, and about meeting our expectation on attendance?"

"You know, I was real busy last night with the company bowling league. We're in first place, you know. But I decided I want to keep my job," Jimmy grinned, "so all you have to do is tell me how much I can be out, and I'm yours."

"Jimmy, who is responsible for your being at work on time?" Marty asked.

"I reckon I am," Jimmy replied cautiously.

"So who's the only person who can improve your performance?" Marty said.

"I don't know if anybody can, since y'all won't tell me how much I can miss," said Jimmy, "and since you're so inconsistent. Chuck can be late and nothing's said to him . . . ."

"That ain't true," Sonny said. "We did talk to Chuck, and he told us specifically what he was committing to do that was gonna fix his problem. On the other hand, you ain't committed to do nothin'."

Marty laid it on the line. "Jimmy, are you prepared to tell us your plan to improve your attendance and meet the expectation?"

"Look, what you see is what you get. It's your job to plan."

"And what's your job, Jimmy?"

"To do what you tell me," Jimmy said.

"And we asked you to come prepared with a plan this morning. Is that what you heard?"

"Yeah, but like I said . . ."

"So, you're telling me that you're not prepared with a

plan to meet the expectation?"

"I reckon not. It ain't fair."

"Then, it's obvious to me that you are unlikely to meet the expectation. Would you agree?"

> Key question: What is the likelihood of lasting improvement?

"You do what you gotta do, and I'll do what I gotta do." Jimmy looked down at the floor, sneaked a peek at Marty under his cap brim, and returned to his downward stare.

"Jimmy, based on your behavior of yesterday toward Sonny and your lack of commitment to meet our expectation on attendance, your employment here is over."

"You can't do that . . ." Jimmy started.

"Jimmy, it's over," Marty said firmly. "The only remaining question is how you want it reflected on your record. Since your reason for dismissal didn't involve gross misconduct or violence, we will offer you a chance to resign if you want."

"What good is that?" Jimmy said, "and what about my unemployment?"

> Maintain respect at termination even for those not deserving it.

"I don't think it's necessary to kick you on your way out," Marty said. "Although your behavior isn't acceptable, you're a person just like me. If it were me, I'd rather tell people I quit and not have to lie about it."

Marilyn finally spoke up. "As far as unemployment, we don't make that determination; the state does. You'll apply for benefits at the state office, and

> Fairness is based on consistency of process, not simply outcome.

they'll ask your reason for leaving. You tell them it's a requested resignation. We'll provide them with information, and they'll decide if your case fits their standards."

"I'm sorry it came to this, Jimmy," said Marty. "Believe it or not, I really am."

ENSURE ACCOUNTABILITY

- A performance problem exists when:
    - ♦ a pattern of misbehavior or poor results continues without sustained improvement
    - ♦ misbehavior is found to be intentional or malicious
    - ♦ a behavior violates laws or shows disrespect for others or the company (fighting, stealing, abusive language)

- To deal with problem behaviors:
    - ♦ Ensure awareness of the problem and understanding of its importance.
    - ♦ Give them a chance to explain; listen actively and ask open-ended questions.
    - ♦ Ask for their commitment to a specific change.
    - ♦ Look for specific action plans that bring intent to life.
    - ♦ Support good-faith tries even if they stumble.

(continued)

- Focus on behavior, not attitude, personality or the past.
- Key question: What is the likelihood of lasting improvement?
- Credible consequences work—emotion doesn't.
- Remember, it's the employee's responsibility to change—not yours.
- Maintain respect even at termination—even for those not deserving it.
- Fairness is based on consistency of process, not simply outcome.

Getting Results

It takes time and effort to create change, but staying the same guarantees failure.

*****

"If you want to run with the big dogs, you gotta get off the porch." —Bubba

32

It had been four months since Jimmy's departure and not quite six since implementing the new approach. Frank the Operations VP and Tom the HR VP were here to check preliminary results.

Several employees, including Bubba and Missy, led a tour for the visitors to show how well the plant was functioning.

Next, the managers met in the training room to review the results of the new attendance policy. "Here's the reason we're ahead of budget," Marty said. "More than 96% at work each day, on time—and those are accurate numbers. More than 47% have perfect attendance for six months. That's a miracle compared to what it was last year."

"How many did you have to fire to get this, Marty?" Tom chimed in sarcastically. He knew the answer, but seemed to revel in the power to ask the question.

"Three employees are no longer working here," Marty replied. "One was dismissed, and two quit voluntarily because they could see that they would not be able to meet our expectation. Also, as I discussed with Frank, the assembly supervisor resigned last week because he wasn't comfortable managing with our new approach. Some habits are hard to break."

"And, sir, if you don't mind my buttin' in," Sonny said, "the ones that left don't explain the turnaround. It's the ones who stayed and improved their performance who's made the difference. This approach makes it easier on those who were always here every day. They can be more productive since they don't have to pick up slack for those who are out."

"You've made quite an improvement," Frank acknowledged. "What's next?"

"Our goal is to sustain attendance at between 98 and 99%, year in and year out. In fact, that isn't a goal; it's an expectation."

"So, based on this 95 and 5 stuff, you just got rid of the 5% that were dragging you down, right?" said Tom.

"No, that's not it at all," Marty said. "We don't put our emphasis on the 5%'s behaviors; we deal with them. We've tried to redesign the system around 95% expectations."

"It's not the majority of the people who are the problem. It's the way we lead people—the systems and procedures which let the 5% control what we can achieve. Our focus is to improve the system for us all by involving the people who know the job best."

After the session, Marty asked Frank and Tom to come to his office. "I'd like to promote Bubba Self to fill our vacancy as Assembly Supervisor."

"Well," Frank said, "that's an interesting choice. He's

the set-up technician, right?"
"Any assembly experience?" asked Tom.
"No. But he has one characteristic that we desperately need: leadership," Marty said. "He's perceptive, he listens well even under pressure, and he has high expectations. Our people respect what he says because they've seen him perform. He's a big reason we've come this far. He learned the machine set-up role very quickly, and I expect he can learn assembly just as quickly."
"It sounds like the right choice to me," Frank said. Tom nodded agreement.
"You've made a great start, Marty," Frank added. "I'm looking forward to seeing how you sustain it."
"That's the challenge," Marty agreed, "but with the 95% involved, I think we can."

33

The next few weeks were busy for Bubba as he learned the new job. As he learned the technical processes of Assembly, Bubba also learned the strengths of each of his employees. His openness, humor, and willingness to listen had earned him respect—even though his occasional mistakes gave his employees something to rib him about.

He'd seen Marty only in the brief production meetings held each Monday morning. He was surprised when Marty appeared, daybook in hand, in the Assembly department one morning.

"Checkin' up on me?" Bubba called.

"Yeah . . . I mean, no—not the way you mean," Marty stammered. "I've been thinking. Frank's right. The real challenge will be to maintain our improvements over a long period. It's easy for people to forget how bad we were, and to take for granted how far we've come."

"Guess you're right," Bubba said. "Whatcha got in the book this time?"

"First, I've tried to summarize what we expect of people," Marty said. "See what you think of this Code of Conduct."

> Each employee, in respecting himself or herself, must also respect the rights and privileges of other employees, customers, and the company--including the need for the company to operate profitably.

"I like that," Bubba replied. "It sorta gives folks one rule to live by."

"That's the idea. I also think I've developed sort of a monitoring system to help keep us on track," Marty said.

"Kinda like an instrument panel—to tell you what's happenin' under the hood?" asked Bubba.

"Yeah. That's a good illustration," Marty said. "Take a look at these 'gauges.'"

The pages read:

GETTING RESULTS 117

> **Six Key Indicators of a Positive Workplace**
> 1. Practice mutual trust and respect
> 2. Maintain personal accountability for doing right
> 3. Identify and eliminate workplace negatives
> 4. Make 2-way communication a priority
> 5. Educate, involve, and empower the 95%
> 6. Provide competitive wages & benefits

"You mean, if we keep on doing these things, we'll have a good place to work?" Bubba asked.

"Yes, I think so," said Marty. "They all tie together. Think about it: Can you hold people accountable for doing right without showing them trust and respect every day? Will people want to learn and be involved if our wages aren't competitive?"

"And listenin' to folks is really the key, I think," said Bubba. "It shows 'em you care about them as people, not just as workers."

"Leaders have to also constantly look for negatives that hold people back from performing their best, too," Marty concluded.

"And the people doin' the job know the job best, like you always told me, so it pays to listen to 'em," Bubba agreed.

Getting Things Done
by Tom Peters

Most grand strategies flop. Most change programs fizzle. Why? We worry too much about the plan—and not enough about implementation. Looking back on 35 or so years of being managed, managing, and observing organizations, I offer a few of the top implementers' secrets:

Listening. You'll invariable find answers—if your ears are open. The average boss is a better talker than listener. On the other hand, peak performers in any role may be close to inarticulate—but they absorb a million details of what's on other folks' minds. Then act accordingly.

Curiosity. Never stop asking: "Can you help me understand this better?" "Can you give me an example" "Can you direct me to the person closest to the action?"

Information. Forget information overload. *All* people crave information and being "in the loop." The informed person is the empowered person. The uninformed person is the unempowered person.

"Talk the walk." You've heard of "walk the talk," but organization researcher Karl Weick insists the reverse is even more important. The leader's chief role is to add coherence to the ambiguous real world. That happens only when the boss hangs out, observes—and then explains, vividly, what she's seen and what it means in the larger scheme of things.

Just do it. The reason most plans are a joke is that, in truth, nobody knows nothin' about nothin'. So the only way we can make any progress is to do something—and then see what happens.

Life is not about serenely walking down the middle of spick-and-span streets. It's about veering to and fro, bouncing off the guardrails, then overcorrecting. But you can't correct a course until you've taken to the road!

"I think you pretty well got it figured out."

"Partly thanks to you," Marty said.

"Folks like me may not be too smooth, but we've seen a thing or two over the years," Bubba said. "I'm real glad we finally got someone to listen."

"I'm just glad I finally got smart enough to listen," Marty thought.

STEPS TO A POSITIVE WORKPLACE	Or as Bubba says . . .
Recognize the impact of the system— • on the decent majority and • on the 5% who are game players.	*Most people want to do what's right, but they get fed up.*
Pursue change— understand that change is a process, not an event.	*Folks ain't opposed to change, when they see what's in it for 'em.*

(continued)

Redesign the system based on high expectations.
- Identify and eliminate negatives in the system
- Demonstrate mutual trust and respect in your actions.
- Create involvement and overcome obstacles through active listening.

Lots of folks want to make things better. They're just waitin' for bosses to listen.

Ensure accountability for doing right— for yourself and others.

If people give better, they oughta get better.

Measure results.
Set tangible targets for improvement:
- attendance
- output/productivity
- waste/errors, service, etc.

If you always do what you've always done, you'll always get what you always got.

Watch six key indicators to keep culture on track:
- Actions that show trust & respect
- Personal accountability
- Identify and eliminate negatives
- Two-way communication
- Employee learning & involvement
- Competitive wages/benefits

You gotta keep paying attention 'cause it ain't ever finished.

Final Thoughts

While some would say that Bubba's wisdom is simple—even simplistic—it is surprisingly difficult to reduce the process of creating a positive workplace to a few "steps." The techniques illustrated in this book are based on a philosophy: that the workplace system must be designed around the interests and concerns of the dependable and conscientious majority of employees, not the malicious 5%.

Philosophies aren't always neat, orderly, or easy to articulate. Obviously, without a deep commitment to your conscientious employees, nothing in the book makes sense. But beliefs must drive action, or they become merely good intentions. For change to be effective, it must address both formal policies and individual behaviors.

It's easy to understate the importance of a system, yet it can facilitate or hinder supervisors in "doing the right thing." Often, organizations train their supervisors and are disappointed with the results—the trained supervisors don't do anything differently. Supervisors would like to apply what they've learned, but existing policies can make it difficult. Similarly, merely changing policies without changing problem behaviors will not change workplace results. It isn't enough to train people; you must also make sure the system supports their efforts.

In short, individual behaviors and the workplace system must complement the 95/5 philosophy in order for the workplace to operate effectively.

Although Bubba's story is underpinned with real incidents, it is fictional; thus, we have included three actual case studies in Appendix B to illustrate how businesses at different locations and times applied these principles successfully.

Appendix A

BUT WHAT ABOUT ... ?

Do these concepts work in the real world?

Yes. The concepts have been around at least since Moses, but we aren't that old. For the past 18 years, we've seen them work in new facilities and existing ones; in previously 'OK' environments as well as in very poor ones. See Appendix B for some details on measurable outcomes. In addition to the dollars-and-cents improvements, you'll notice subtle differences in workplace behaviors—people helping others without being asked, and offering ideas and committing to work on them.

What are the keys to success?

First, leaders have to approach the concepts as values to be lived out, not as a "program" to fix something broken. You have to genuinely believe that the vast majority of people want to do a good job, and make your decisions based on that belief. That's not as easy as it sounds. You can't fake it; people can smell a phony. Second, it helps to have a reasonably healthy market forecast for your product for the coming months. It sounds a bit hollow to talk about mutual respect when you're routinely laying off employees. Finally, if your work relationships are in deep trouble now, you will need to build bridges first—don't try to make these changes in the midst of a strike, for example. No one will believe you're sincere, and you may run afoul of laws.

How long does it take?
We can't generalize. It depends on how good or bad the environment is, how committed the leadership team is, how much investment can be dedicated to it, how flexible the work process is to allow employee involvement, and so on. As the story indicated, you can see results from little improvements almost immediately upon implementation. Bigger changes (like attendance) take more time to plan and get approvals, but once implemented, get results almost immediately. Most should see a big difference in six months to a year.

I like some of the ideas in the book, but others I question. Is it an all-or-nothing deal?
No. We've never had a client who has taken all of our ideas and implemented them.

Part of it depends on what you feel are the biggest 'hurts' you have. The real goal is for each organization to examine their own practices in light of the Six Key Indicators on page 117. Then, you decide what needs to be changed. One hint: The more people you can involve, the more buy-in and trust you build—the less time it will take.

Specialty Products didn't have a union. Will these concepts work with unionized employees?
Yes. People are people; despite stereotypes, most union members are 95%-ers.

We've seen success in unionized facilities, but involvement of the local union leadership is key, even if the changes won't affect terms that are negotiable. Leaders are still responsible for determining how they will treat people—as badly as they are legally permitted, or with the respect they want themselves. We've found that, when you ask managers and union leaders separately what kind of workplace they want, their answers are the same. Some of the processes you use will differ. You can adapt them to the situation.

This stuff sounds too soft. You don't know the kind of people we have—they'll only give the minimum.
You're right; we don't know the people you work with, but we'd still bet that the majority of your coworkers at all levels are decent human beings. Some of them may have given up a little self-respect because the system made that a rational choice. And it's true that society has changed in recent years. Personal accountability isn't automatically instilled at home or school anymore, so we have to establish it at work. Again, though, our experience suggests that the vast majority of people entering the workforce are basically decent, and will respond with their best efforts for a company that treats them with respect. You will have to help the minority who won't make or keep commitments find a way to change, or find a way out.

One last point: Don't misunderstand 'respect' to mean 'permissiveness.' Sometimes the most respectful thing you can do is tell a person his or her behavior is out of bounds and can't continue. In a positive workplace, you set high standards and hold people to them. A positive workplace isn't an easy place to work.[1]

I like the ideas, but corporate won't let me . . . the union won't let me . . . my boss won't let me . . .
We get the picture. What was it Bubba said—"It's easy to find reasons not to do something"? All authority is delegated from somewhere, and no manager is free to do whatever he or she wants. However, you can control how you will treat

people personally. Start by removing some annoyances that keep people from doing a good job.

> "A journey of 1000 miles begins with a single step."

Appendix B

CASE STUDIES

The principles portrayed in *Bubba on Business* have been successfully utilized by actual companies to create effective environments and improved business results. Here are some brief profiles of real clients from different industries and points in time, presented anonymously.

Apparel manufacturing operation, 400+ employees, nonunion (Tennessee, 1982)

Situation. All operating indicators were negative—the facility was losing $100,000/month; absenteeism was 8–10% daily; turnover was 125% annualized; the lost time accident rate was high.

Analysis. A very benevolent but paternalistic culture created distrust between employees and management. Management selectively applied policies. Previously, management had attempted to improve attendance with a "bonus" of 30¢ per hour if an individual had perfect attendance for only a week. However, individuals with attendance problems were allowed to repeat the cycle (absences—discipline—improvement—discipline removed—more absences) for years. Compounding the high turnover rate, employees were rehired after quitting without notice—up to five times in some cases. Incentives were offered for employees to refer relatives and friends; incentives were paid for referrals if new employees lasted as little as a week.

Actions taken. A new Director of Operations and Human Resources Manager introduced the 95/5 philosophy to leaders with a one-day orientation. Structured weekly and monthly communication forums with hourly employees were established. The early focus of these sessions was to (1) identify issues that diminished productivity and respect; (2) begin communicating the philosophy; and (3) establish higher expectations regarding performance.

Next, leaders were trained in communication skills and performance counseling (the disciplinary method Marty and Bubba outlined in the book). Thus equipped, leaders began to identify out-of-bounds behaviors and to address individual examples. Expectations were communicated, commitment sought, and common-sense consequences developed. For example, under the new policies, quitting without notice made an individual ineligible for rehire.

Employee-involvement activities helped create ownership of the process. An employee-management policy review team recommended changes oriented toward the 95% rather than the 5%. A Safety Committee took on the long-standing problem of lost-time accidents. An ongoing leadership development curriculum enhanced leaders' skills.

Results. Productivity improved 12%. Damage rate (defects due to manufacturing) were reduced from 12% to under 3%. Attendance improved to more than 98%. Turnover was reduced to less than 25% annualized. The facility received national recognition for safety, achieving 2.75 million hours without a lost-time accident (a period of 2.5 years). Although operated as a cost center, the facility contributed over $1 million to the corporate bottom line annually.

Plastic injection molding operation, 500 employees, unionized (Ohio, 1993)

Situation. In 1993, and previously, absenteeism averaged over 8% daily. Local union leaders had complained to management that "absenteeism is killing us." The parties agreed to explore new options for handling absenteeism.

Analysis. Both management and union leaders knew that their previous system was not working, but had never seen any alternative. When they met initially, they discussed approaches taken by other companies—none of which were better than their own. Still, they were initially resistant to a policy which did not draw a line. Ninety-Five/Five, Inc. led the group through the thought process outlined in Chapter 17 of this book.

Actions taken. Ninety-Five/Five, Inc. trained a policy-review team consisting of members from the union and the company to design a new attendance approach. To overcome fears of favoritism, a joint review committee of labor and management was established to review anonymous attendance calendars monthly, ask questions regarding reasons and previous actions, and recommend where action needed to be taken. All supervisors and shop stewards/union committee members received training in the attendance approach and the disciplinary process that accompanied it. Group meetings with all employees were held to announce the changes that were implemented by management as a work rule. Individual precounseling sessions were held with individuals who would likely have a problem under the new approach.

Results. The planning, communicating, and policy changes took about nine months to finalize. Immediately upon implementation, attendance improved to about 98% and has remained steady at that level.

Warehouse distribution operation, 1200 employees, nonunion (Indiana, 1997)

Situation. Absenteeism was 10% or higher, especially on Mondays and Fridays which were the heaviest workdays. Turnover was approximately 80 employees each month. Some supervisors had groups of 80 employees spread out over thousands of square feet—keeping track of everyone was a nightmare.

Analysis. The employees could not leave work at the end of each day until all the trucks were loaded—so those present on Mondays and Fridays could look forward to 12-hour days. This, and management's inability to hold people accountable, led some good employees to quit, even though the wages were good for the area. The high turnover and high absenteeism created tremendous stress for Human Resources and the supervisors.

Action taken. After initial contact with us, a team was formed to review the attendance policy only. We provided one day of training and orientation. The team chose to proceed with the "every day, on time" expectation. Next, training in the new policy and in performance counseling was provided to all supervisors.

Results. Attendance improved to over 97% upon implementation and has remained at that level. Supervisors report that turnover has slowed. "About 30" total employees left apparently as a result of the new approach; three were dismissed; and the others left voluntarily after making and breaking commitments for improvement.

Appendix C

MEASURABLE RESULTS

How can you objectively measure progress in creating an effective workplace? Obviously, gains in morale are subjective and intangible, but they're clearly visible—especially when you have problems.

One area that most companies can measure is attendance; however, it isn't as easy as you think to compare apples to apples. You see, many companies don't "count" every absence—it's tough to think about how bad things really are.

For example, some point systems give only one point to an individual who misses two or more consecutive days. This policy is intended to keep from penalizing people who are legitimately sick, with the idea that "real" illnesses will last more than one day. However, they end up penalizing people who try to come back from an illness too early and relapse. Other companies institute mini-leaves for the same reason: Each day counts as a point, unless you miss five days in a row; then, it counts as zero. If you had to be out a couple of days, would the rational choice be to come back to work the next day under that system? And some no-fault systems really aren't no-fault, because they require a doctor's note to excuse an absence.

All of the above policies came about when a hard-nosed system negatively impacted a good performer, and the organization believed an exception was needed. You can see the problem for measurement. It's hard to get a true baseline when you switch from a system which doesn't count some absences to one that records every absence on scheduled work days (exceptions are bereavement; jury/civic duty and vacations—because attendance is not scheduled; absences on overtime are counted, because it's scheduled work time) and looks for patterns of abuse instead of incidents or occurrences.

Even with these difficulties, it's still possible to measure attendance improvement in many organizations.

Another objective measurement of progress is turnover—people are more likely to stay at a workplace which treats them as responsible adults. Turnover is a bit more complex than attendance, because there are many good reasons someone might leave a company—moving from the area; change in family circumstances (for instance, divorce, marriage, spouse's promotion, or the birth of a child); need for a different work schedule; military service or educational opportunity; an industry that's up-and-down; even a mid-life crisis. "More money" is often cited as a reason for leaving, but our experience is that, in many cases, it's just a socially acceptable excuse. The real question for a company is, "Why were they looking?" While money is important to everyone, we see countless cases where people leave higher paying jobs to come to work in a positive environment where the pay may be less. As one such interviewee said, "We've finally figured it out—they're paying us more than the job is worth so they can treat us like crap."* (On the other hand, you can't pay the lowest possible wages and have a positive environment—look at the last Key Indicator on page 117.)

Certainly, "treating people the way you want to be treated" is more than an economic issue. However, business legitimately uses dollars to measure value—and clearly, by that measure, there are tangible rewards for improving the workplace environment.

Appendix D

WAYS TO GET STARTED

Obviously, each business is different. Where and how you start to implement changes depends on your history of trust or distrust, your company's "personality," the problems you face, the resources you have, and many other factors. Here's a list of ideas—some risky, some tame; some difficult, some easy—that others have used to start the change process by creating awareness and developing understanding.

- Have your leadership team read this book, then discuss it. Evaluate your organization against the Six Key Indicators on page 117. Ask your fellow employees some key questions like:
    - ♦ What percentage of people do you really believe are basically decent?
    - ♦ Who do you think our company policies are most designed for: the 95% or the 5%?
    - ♦ Do you feel that the company really treats most people like responsible adults? Do most of our people deserve to be treated like adults?
    - ♦ Are there some people who always try to take advantage of situations? Are they mostly the same people?
    - ♦ How committed do you think they are to their jobs? What should we do with those people?
    - ♦ Should everybody be treated equally, regardless of their past behaviors?

- Start a series of skip-level meetings with employees. Listen to the negatives that concern them.

  One caveat: If you haven't done this before, you're likely to hear a lot of trivial issues, impossible demands, and hostility designed to test your commitment. Don't make commitments for change too hastily. Instead, listen and ask why these are important. This stage will pass and people will move to more basic issues.

- Identify one major issue involving people that, if solved, would dramatically impact your bottom line. Brainstorm unconventional ways to tackle this based on Bubba's principles.

- Conduct an employee opinion survey—but only if you're willing to report results honestly and act on the things you discover.

- Walk around the facility. Find some 95%-ers and ask each of them about "the one thing you would do if you were plant manager."

- Eat lunch at a large table in the break room or cafeteria once a week. Each week, specifically invite a new group of employees to join you. Talk about orders, customers, new products and equipment—or just what people have done today at work. Listen to the questions they ask and topics they bring up.

- Have an off-site meeting for your managers and, if unionized, the union committee. Discuss what kind of workplace you really want, and what obstacles are in your way.

- Assemble a policy-review team to look at one of your major policies (like attendance or discipline) or your entire handbook. Ask, "How would I feel if this were applied to me?" Look for policies designed around the 5%, and refocus them on the 95%.

> "The best time to plant a tree was 20 years ago. The second best time is today."
> —Chinese proverb

- If you decide to change a major policy, talk individually with as many people as you can. Discuss how the change would affect them. Discuss concerns honestly; ask them for support.
- Identify one or more bottom performers. Analyze what behaviors they display, how those differ from expectations, and what consequences they have gotten for them. Develop a plan to meet with them and discuss changes they are willing to make.

Who Wrote This Book?

Ninety-Five/Five, Incorporated—named after the 95/5 principle—is a leadership development company based in Nashville, Tennessee. It was established in 1979, and has worked with companies in 23 states and Canadian provinces to implement changes based on these concepts.

David Dunn is President of Ninety-Five/Five, and the source of many of the book's examples and situations. He draws on his experience with dozens of clients as a consultant, first with The Thompson Group and then with Ninety-Five/Five, plus his years as an operations manager and a Human Resources director in a production environment.

Dennis Melton is Vice President of Ninety-Five/Five, and developed the book's story, characters and dialogue. Prior to becoming a principal in Ninety-Five/Five, he worked in organization development and employee/leadership communications for a major telecom equipment manufacturer, and in video, advertising and marketing for a satellite system manufacturer and a nonprofit organization.

To contact the authors: Send an e-mail to: bubba@95-5.com or call (615) 831-9505. For more information, visit the authors' Web page at www.95-5.com.

For information about purchasing additional copies and bulk discounts, contact the authors, your local bookstore, or the publisher.

RELATED BOOKS BY SELECT PRESS

Thriving on Change in Organizations
edited by Rick Crandall

"This could be the best book on change....Managers can't be 'dummies'. The biggest part of managing today is dealing with change, and this book will make you lots smarter."
— Bob Nelson, author, *1001 Ways to Reward Employees* and co-author, *Managing for Dummies*

Rapid change is here to stay. Those businesses and organizations that don't adapt to the new environment will be left behind. **Thriving on Change** shows business owners, managers, and executives how it is possible to not only adapt to change but to *thrive* on it. Specific insights from 14 experts from around the country will help readers pave their paths to success in the '90s. Plus an easy-to-read design.

Paperback, 316 pages • ISBN: 0-9644294-5-4 • Price: $17.95

Break-Out Creativity: Bringing Creativity to the Workplace
edited by Rick Crandall

"Fun to read, practical, and results-oriented....Open the book to any page and you'll discover something that will help you become more creative and innovative today."
— Michael Michalko, author, *Thinkertoys*

Break-Out Creativity will help you and your organization be more creative. Creativity is the ability to look at your world in new ways. Innovation is the *application* of creativity to produce results. Ten experts help you understand and apply creativity to produce new results, and results is what this book is all about! Opening up the doors of your mind is enjoyable. And the format of this book is playful, fun, and easy to read or skim. Turn to any page and you'll see an idea, an example, or a graphic that brings creativity and innovation alive for you right now.

Paperback, 170 pages • ISBN: 0-9644294-7-0 • Price: $14.95

SELECT PRESS • P.O. BOX 37 • CORTE MADERA, CA 94976-0037 • (415) 435-4461

ASSESSMENT CENTERS
Research & Applications

"Riggio and Mayes have done an outstanding job in documenting the existing research and the many applications of the assessment center. The editors have gathered a virtual *Who's Who* of assessment centers....The result is an outstanding overview of many facets of the assessment center, including a superb recounting of its history and an insightful prognosis for its use in the 21st century. Answers to all the critical questions...are provided by the outstanding group of practitioners/researchers the editors have assembled."

—Randall Schuler, PhD
Professor, Leonard N. Stern School of Business
New York University

"...a must read and valuable reference for human resource practitioners, applied psychologists, and professionals in educational evaluation....an up-to-date, highly authoritative examination of an important method for employee selection and development. The articles explain the merit of assessment centers for organizations today, especially their value in measuring aspects of interpersonal relationships that cannot be measured readily in other ways, such as surveys. Articles cover the science and practice of assessment centers and show the creative use of assessment methods in a variety of organizational and educational settings."

—Manuel London, PhD
Professor and Director
Center for Human Resource Management
State University of New York at Stony Brook
and former human resources manager at AT&T

"...must reading for both assessment center researchers and practitioners. The papers by Bray & Byham, Howard, and Lowry do a wonderful job of establishing a useful context for looking at the past and future of assessment centers. The set of articles on construct validity of assessment centers provides valuable insight to both researchers interested in developing better theories of why assessment centers work, and to practitioners looking for opportunities to improve."

—Richard J. Ritchie, PhD
AT&T Assessment Services Director
Morristown, New Jersey

Assessment Centers: Research & Applications. Edited by Ronald E. Riggio & Bronston T. Mayes. A special issue of the *Journal of Social Behavior and Personality*, 1997, Vol. 12, No. 5. (338 pp, $30, ISBN 1-890777-02-1)

SELECT PRESS • P.O. BOX 37 • CORTE MADERA, CA 94976-0037 • (415) 435-4461

MORE TOOLS FROM THE AUTHORS OF *BUBBA*

Create a workplace that gets results

How do you help your people perform their best?
How many times have you invested in training, only to have leaders act the same afterward. Did you ever consider . . .

Maybe they need more than just training—they need tools.
It isn't enough to train poeple to behave differently—you need to support their behaviors with procedures and practices.

They need the *Leadership Procedures Guide* to create a workplace that gets results.

Leadership Procedures Guide Features

- ✔ Over 60 prototype procedures, ready to select and customize
- ✔ Essential forms, ready to use!
- ✔ Unique, effective positive workplaces methods—uses high expectations instead of rules which try to control misbehavior
- ✔ Can be installed over a network for online access by leaders
- ✔ Built-in interactive links—one-click access from index to policy!
- ✔ Built-in, preformatted header on each policy to capture required data
- ✔ WordPerfect™ or MS Word™ editable
- ✔ Multi-location discounts available
- ✔ Includes FREE editable **Employee Handbook** prototype

Includes binder with printed copy of all policies and 4 diskettes. Price: $900 (a 50% discount is available when other services are purchased)

For orders & information:
Ninety-Five/Five, Inc.
(615) 831-9505 or www.95-5.com

Ninety-Five-Five, Inc. is a leadership development firm and does not offer legal advice. Users assume all responsibility for determining whether these practices are applicable to their workplaces, and all risk from implementation. State laws differ, and the prototypes may not fit all situations.